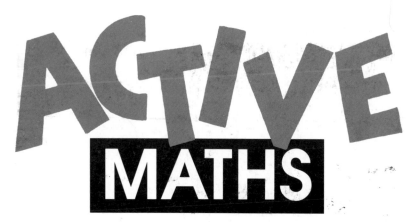

ACTIVE MATHS

PRIMARY MATHS FROM THE ENVIRONMENT

A teacher's book
from the
World Wide Fund for Nature

Margaret Williams
Toni McPherson
Margaret Mackintosh
Michael Williams

CONTENTS

INTRODUCTION

The National Curriculum has defined the mathematical content for Key Stage One. This book provides a series of environmentally linked contexts, which are realistic, meaningful and enjoyable, for the learning and teaching of much of that mathematics.

Environmental education, discussed in Curriculum Guidance 7, is one of the five cross-curricular themes identified by the National Curriculum Council.

The seven Themes in this book are based on the seven topics or areas of knowledge identified in Curriculum Guidance 7 as pre-eminent in education about the environment. It is felt that this should make the ideas in the book more readily accessible to teachers, many of whom will have planned other parts of the curriculum around these topics.

Using this book children will be learning IN the environment, THROUGH the environment, ABOUT the environment and FOR the environment.

There has developed a realisation, which year by year becomes more convincing, that the quality of life for present and future generations will depend upon awareness of the environment, the effect it has upon us and the effect we have upon it. Talking about the environment is a step in the right direction: working in the environment and with the environment must communicate a more personal and effective message.

The National Curriculum Council makes the affirmation that, "A coherent cross-curricular curriculum helps pupils to make connections between different parts of their studies and between these and the world in which they live".

Whilst accepting that it is important to raise children's awareness of the environment, this does not mean that they should be frightened or made over-anxious by emphasis on 'doom and gloom'. Rather it is deemed sufficient that consideration of 'problems' and 'issues' should be set at a level commensurate with children's comprehension, avoiding the unreasonable burden of whole-world issues and incomprehensible timescales.

The preferred emphasis will be on the enjoyment, appreciation and wise use of the environment and its bounty as first steps towards the development of mature sensibilities and an active, caring concern in the future.

some general observations

Please read the whole book before starting on any individual theme.

Some skills or processes described in one place may be necessary or useful elsewhere. It is also important, because of the close weave of environmental studies, to know what appears in other sections so that opportunities are not duplicated or wasted.

Since it covers such a wide range of interests this book cannot claim to offer a complete and fully detailed guide to all the possible activities in each theme. It does assume a significant working partnership with the teachers' considerable contribution of skill and professional expertise.

The material in this book is not set forward as a teaching scheme nor does it attempt to constrain any teacher to a rigid order of use. Each section can be considered as a free-standing unit and be used as and when the teacher feels that it suits the pupils' needs, current circumstances or topical opportunities. Because of the all-embracing character and essential homogeneity of environmental relationships, teachers could decide to select aspects from different sections and re-combine them to suit specific contexts (fitting in with a major whole-school theme), or to create a more personal choice of emphasis.

In most cases the text describes **what to do** but not **how to do it** because of the confidence that teachers will bring their own talents, expertise and experience to the tasks. Teachers will interpret the ideas to suit their own children, the children's other studies and the particular locality.

format and organisation

As far as possible a common format has been used for each section. After a brief INTRODUCTION some DISCUSSION POINTS are suggested in the form of questions which the teacher could use with the children. The questions are not only or explicitly mathematical. They are broadly based and while they serve to open up the topic they could also serve as a useful indicator of the children's current knowledge and understanding of the theme. The major part of each section consists of suggestions for a range of essentially mathematical ACTIVITIES which start with PLAY or EXPLORATION and gradually become more specific and more challenging. Indications of possible ASSESSMENTS follow the activities with suggestions for further development through CROSS-CURRICULAR and HOME/SCHOOL LINKS. Each section ends with an INVESTIGATION posed as a question.

We hope you will find the text easy to follow, use and adapt. We would like to think that you will wish to repeat the activities, and to this end we recommend that you continue to add to collections and other resources and keep notes of your experiences so that each repetition will be easier and even more successful than the previous one. Each section includes a page for your personal records so that they may be kept conveniently and safely.

This is not a mathematics 'text book for teachers'. The final chapter does, however, set out in brief form some of the practices and processes mentioned in the text, as well as discussing the developmental order of some of the handling data skills to provide a convenient source of reference and information.

Some sections have a paragraph labelled RESOURCES AND PREPARATION. This has only been included where the requirements are thought to be substantially different from those usually available within the classroom. The need to organise or assemble other specific resources and make suitable preparations will be related by teachers to their individual plans for the work.

the activities

Many of the themes have much more potential for mathematical and other activities than has been described in the text. The aim has been to define starting points and experiences which provide for a broad range of abilities, including possibilities for stretching and stimulating the most able children. Therefore the choice of suitable levels of use and selection will always be left to the discretion of the teacher.

It is not expected that these themes and activities will cater for all the necessary aspects of mathematics teaching. It is intended that the maths will arise from the studies of the environment. The environment theme has not been manipulated just to squeeze in an unnecessary or inappropriate piece of mathematics. It is recognised that other elements of mathematics will need to be continued alongside these studies.

In some cases activities will have been numbered or lettered for convenience of presentation. This does not always imply a preferred or essential sequencing, and elements could be restructured differently although in some instances one piece of work does depend upon another.

Because of the pragmatic nature of much of the work which is suggested, there is a great emphasis on PROCESS involving both practical and intellectual skills. One of the virtues of such work is that it removes the expectation of standard algorithms and 'sums with right answers'.

assessment

As the main intention of this book is mathematical, reference is made throughout to the most likely areas of content for specific assessment. Opportunities for the assessment of children's skill in "Using and applying mathematics" (NAT 1) are present in all activities. No attempt has been made to provide assessment guidance in other study areas.

home/school links

The HOME/SCHOOL LINKS activities are mathematically rich and considered to be integral parts of the main Theme: as such they should be followed up when the work comes into school. They should be seen as important, and signals of that importance conveyed to parents.

Many schools have well-established and carefully structured patterns of parental involvement and the values of these, to children, parents and teachers, are convincingly documented. If your school is not yet in that position, these studies make an excellent starting point. Much of the information and data required can only be obtained from the home and with the parents' co-operation, giving a special and recognisable validity and uniqueness to the home contribution.

cross-curricular links

The text suggests some of the natural and convenient links but does not aim to include all the possibilities, and avoids creating tenuous or spurious links. Therefore, some sections and some subjects have more links than others.

investigations

The investigations provide opportunities for children to work co- operatively in pairs or groups.

It does not seem necessary to overload the sections with multiple INVESTIGATIONS and it is impossible to anticipate the wide variations in potential treatments of the material by different schools or groups of children. It is hoped that, accepting the principles stated, teachers will generate other investigations appropriate to their own experiences, or facilitate the work of their pupils by offering them a range of investigations which would adapt to their abilities and interests.

Since the investigations are open-ended and encourage individual thinking, actions and conclusions, they can be used to assess NAT 1 and another NAT at the same time which will provide evidence of differentiated assessment.

The investigations which come at the end of each section are posed as questions from a member of a 'family' of people. This is intended to take the enquiry role away from the teacher to someone else with a genuine curiosity to whom the information, thinking and conclusion of the answer must be communicated.

The teacher's expectations of the children's responses to the investigations will be tailored to the known ability of individual pupils. Generally a simple 'yes' or 'no' would not be considered satisfactory, so the initial question is followed by the demand for evidence or proof. It is more in this area that children should be encouraged to develop convincing reasoning backed by their evidence or experience of the activities.

The manner and quality of the presentation of the answer may vary considerably. From one child or group an oral explanation might be acceptable, whereas another may produce evidence using a wide range of skills and techniques using writing, drawings, charts, diagrams, photographs, audio/video tapes etc. This will encourage the best from each child.

mathematics and play

Each of the sections in this book begins with **PLAY** or **EXPLORATION.**

The two terms are seen as interchangeable in their intent and effect. In some situations one may seem more appropriate than the other but the essential character and importance of the activities are the same and have the same vital role within the curriculum.

In common with most other young animals play is the way in which children start their education. Initially they learn about themselves and their immediate environment, but the process continues and develops to include the complexities of more sophisticated social interaction and wider, more generalised contexts.

In a very specific way play is the beginning of mathematical understanding. Play provides opportunities for young children to learn by active and direct participation in concrete situations where the basis of problem solving and creative thinking is established.

Young children have a very limited capacity for dealing with abstractions. Play involves them in a variety of problem solving activities which enable them to make connections, see patterns, create hypotheses, develop theories and organise constructs. It also allows them to imitate the adult world and, through playing out what they see, make meaning of that world.

Play needs to be planned and purposeful in terms of the provision of materials and equipment, the adult's awareness of the learning potential in the play experience, and in the operation of the adult role in realising the potential.

The experiences of young children do not come in packages with subject labels attached, but as they play and explore the world the diverse experiences will include mathematical ones.

Mathematics is integral to children's play just as play is integral to children's acquisition of mathematics.

If children are to develop their mathematical understanding through play, the teacher and other interested adults need to develop and extend the play situations. They should intervene at appropriate times by encouraging, demonstrating or assisting but should not impose their own choices or dominate the actions.

Children should be encouraged to plan their play activity, by discussing what they intend or by defining their proposals through drawing, painting or writing. Similarly, after play they should review their activities by talking about what happened and why.

Children do not make distinctions between play and work. Engrossed in play they are highly motivated and happily persist with activities. In this way they develop their powers of concentration and perseverance.

visits

Studying and learning from the environment must depend significantly on first hand experience of the environment. The immediate environments of home and school do not present much difficulty of access, but widening the horizon to the neighbourhood and beyond usually requires more elaborate planning and organisation. Nevertheless the value of these visits – if they are successfully pursued – can be very substantial and it is to be hoped that all children will be able to enjoy and profit from regular opportunities for study beyond the classroom door and the school gate.

Each visit poses its unique mathematical and other characteristics but much of the basic planning process has been detailed in the section on WATER. Much of that information will be appropriate to other visits but has not been repeated. When visits are being planned it may be useful to refer to this section. Teachers may find it advantageous to extend these notes into a personal 'planning' document and check list or flow diagram to simplify other visits. Through all these procedures due regard should be paid to any Local Authority guidelines on visits.

Much stress has been placed on the importance of the children's participation in the planning process and the point made that, in an ideal situation, they should feel that they are **going** on their visit not being **taken** on someone else's.

The value of children participating in the mathematical aspects of the planning cannot be over-emphasised.

animals - regulations and precautions

In recent years there has been much discussion about the place of animals in classrooms, relating both to their care and to possible health risks to children.

Whilst there would still appear to be a strong consensus of opinion that involvement with animals is desirable, beneficial and rewarding for most young people there is evidence that there are also potential problems.

Certain possibilities have been suggested and teachers are strongly advised to seek local official guidance regarding animals, the handling of soils and their collection.

Some Local Authorities have set out clear instructions or guidelines which it would be unwise to ignore. In addition much good advice about keeping and caring for animals is available from various sources, including the Royal Society For The Protection of Animals.

computers

Reference has been made in the text to the use of computers and in particular to the creation and use of databases. Because of the level and diversity of computer provision and software availability this has not been detailed, but rather left to the teacher's judgement in relating suggestions to their own situation.

calculators

It is assumed that all children will have free access to calculators. Their use builds confidence, removes the distraction of computation at times when the process of enquiry is more important, increases children's fascination with the world of mathematics, and facilitates their understanding of the environment.

investigations illustrations

As mentioned in the introduction (and illustrated occasionally within the text) the investigations are intended to be put to the children as questions from a 'relative', "My Gran says....", "My Uncle wants to know...." etc.

To strengthen this image of an 'outside' enquirer, teachers are invited to use photocopies of the following illustrations to construct their own investigation prompts for display to the children.

BUILDINGS, INDUSTRIALISATION AND WASTE

introduction

In the following text the three aspects have been to some extent separated. Since they inter-relate very strongly it will often be convenient to respond to the natural integration. There is a substantial body of activities and studies in this section. Teachers may wish to consider its subdivision into smaller bites to be digested at different times.

This section starts from children's experience and limited knowledge of familiar buildings and making processes, and creates opportunities through which they will deepen their understanding.

They will also have opportunities to extend their perception and appreciation of broader concepts about buildings and how they are constructed and used; about the world of work, and the impact of technology and industrialisation upon their lives and the environment.

Much attention will be paid to the development of the oral and written language required to express their ideas effectively in the associated mathematical activities and processes.

discussion points

buildings

Where do you spend your nights? What do you like about your bedroom? What are the differences between school and home? Why are they different? What other kinds of buildings are there? What do we use buildings for? Are they all the same size/shape? How did they get there? How long will they stay there? How do people make buildings? What tools do they use? What sort of machines do they use? Why do they need machines? What buildings will we see if we walk to the supermarket/church/bus station? In which order will we pass them? Which building will have the most people in it? Will any of the buildings be closed? Are there any buildings we are not allowed to enter?

industrialisation

Who do you pretend you are when you play games? Do you go to work? What do you do at work? Why do people work? Who did you see on the way to school? What were they doing? Do you see the same people every day? What is your favourite meal? How does it get to your table? Which workers helped to make your meal possible? Where does the money come from to pay for the shopping? Who grew/made the ingredients for your food?

waste

What do we throw away after a meal? What did we throw away in preparing the meal? What happens to the things we throw away? How much do we throw away each week at home/at school? What are the things that we throw away regularly/occasionally? What else could we do with the things we don't want/need? How much do we pay for waste (drink containers, sweet wrappers etc)? Can we distinguish between necessary/useful/functional packaging and excessive/wasteful packaging?

activities

1 **Playing** at building
2 **Exploring** the environment
3 **Exploring** our school
4 **Looking** at walls, windows and interiors
5 **Looking** at machinery and gadgets
6 **Looking** at the food we eat
7 **Exploring** industrialisation and waste through what we wear

resources and preparations

Acquire a local street map. Your local Planning Department or neighbourhood Estate Agents may be helpful in this context. Try to obtain copies of the Architect's drawings of your school. Build up a bank of local photographs and/or make a video showing architectural features and their relation to geometric shapes 2D/3D, building uses, different materials and finishes, construction details (include industrial and commercial premises if possible). Several views of the same building can be useful for analysis. Note any litter bins, re-cycling collection points etc and any evidence of waste which has been discarded or dumped. If possible visit a building site observing machinery, equipment and activities. Repeat visit over a period — a note of the timescale can be instructive as well as interesting. Collect examples of building materials. (Try builders's yards and builders' merchants as well as building sites.)

information

The patterns (bonds) in brickwork are standard and may be identified and named by reference to books or builders. Bricks, tiles and paving blocks are interesting examples of functional, albeit irregular, tessellation. It may be useful to consider Primary (producing), Secondary (processing) and Tertiary (servicing) industries.

1 playing at building

Children should have the opportunity to explore the properties of materials used for building and opportunities to create items of their own design. The discussion with other children and adults during play will introduce the mathematics.

Ask the children to choose a sequence of occupational roles and act out/illustrate/write about some of the characteristic activities of these people. These role plays should encourage a consideration of a wide range of occupations and could be limited to that but might, at a later stage, provide data for listing and sorting.

Planning, reviewing and recording activities will also generate opportunities and needs for mathematics.

building

Activities can be centred on the use of real bricks, if available, or the standard building systems such as Community Bricks, Lego, Poleidoblocs, Mini-Quadro, Clixi, Meccano, Cuisenaire (Color factor) and Multilink. Junk materials may be a useful alternative or supply potential details for use with other components and can supply the stimulus for much language development.

When they construct buildings using different materials:
★   Can the children find out which shapes will/will not build a wall?
★   Can the children make a tall building? Which material will build the tallest tower?
★   Can the children record their building on a piece of paper so that someone else can build an identical model?
★   Can the children build a wall on an uneven or sloping surface? (on a school field for example)

While not actually telling the children how to record their buildings (they should always be encouraged to invent their own methods of recording), you may find it useful to make available paper which reflects the units used for building eg. 2 cm squares for Multilink, 1 cm squares for Cuisenaire.

These constructional activities should be followed by discussions with the children about:
★   The materials they have chosen
★   Any handling or constructional/assembly problems experienced
★   Their reasons for choice of design
★   What the building would be used for
★   Which people would work in the building
★   How many people would work in it .... and so on.

Other activities may be based on 'junk box' constructions using salvaged materials to construct buildings, machines or equipment. Alternatively, items which are more commonly considered 'waste' (milk bottle tops, crisp packets, sweet wrappers, yogurt cartons etc) could be used to make a 'Waste Person', using as many different items as possible. The resulting figures could make a useful and illuminating centrepiece for a display.

changing buildings

Sometimes a book will give stimulus to an activity. For instance, the book 'Changes ' by Pat Hutchins could be read to the children as an introduction to the following exercises.

Using small table-top building bricks, create a simple building similar to one shown in the book and ask the children to:

1.   Copy the building
2.   Make a new building using exactly the same blocks.
3.   Record their buildings by drawings or by using rubber stamps.

assessment

Shape & Space:
Talk about models they have made.
Use mathematical terms to describe common 2D and 3D objects.
Length:
Compare and order models without measuring.

cross-curricular links

Art/English:
Record their buildings by drawing or writing about them. They may also be encouraged to write about their experience of and response to the activity.
Technology:
Make your own 'den'.

investigation

Azra says...

Which shapes will build a wall?

Show me how you know.

2 exploring the environment

routes and structures

Take the children for a walk in the vicinity of the school. The children can sketch, take photographs or even make a video film as they go around. Discussion may be directed to ideas about the ORDER in which buildings are passed; the relative SIZES of buildings, the PROPORTIONS of tall/thin, short/fat buildings, the SHAPES of buildings (note roofs) and the NUMBERS of doors, windows or other important features. It may also be interesting to speculate about or observe the people and activities in the buildings.

door numbers

While on the walk study and compare the numbering systems in several roads. When looking for patterns odd and even numbers can be discussed. Other discussion points could include:

★   Why is there a 2a in this street?
★   Why is there no 13 in this street?
★   Why do these street numbers start at 8?
★   Why do 1 & 3, on one side take you further down the street than 2, 4, 6, & 8 on the other side?

modelling

Back in the classroom the children can make a 3D model of their environment. They should make sure that, where possible, the buildings are made and placed to demonstrate approximate proportion, and finished to indicate the texture and character of the building material used.

home school link

Ask the children to record in some way the buildings they pass from school to home, and share their observations with the class by describing as a sequence: "First I passed, then .... etc linking their record to the large scale street map.

street map, places and routes

The children will be interested to study the large scale street map of the area, especially if they can identify their homes, the shops and many of the other buildings which they will have noticed on their walk. They can place cubes on the map to identify these places.

Either use the 3D model of the locality, or, when they become familiar with the street map they can take turns to plan routes to the post office from school, to their friend's house from their house etc. If there is more than one way, can the children identify the shortest?

The children can write a list of directions for a route of their choice from one landmark to another, and give the list to a friend who needs to be able to follow the same route. (Tracing or some similar thin paper laid over a map may be a useful means of checking the routes without spoiling the map.)

sorting

Using the drawings or photographs of the buildings ask the children to sort them by criteria such as, "You buy sweets there" or "It's used most on Sundays." This activity should help children identify that buildings are made for different purposes or serve different functions.

playing

Games can be played such as "I spy". Each child has a turn at silently identifying a building on the model or from the photo collection, whilst the other children ask questions in order to discover which building is being thought of. These questions must be phrased so that they only require a YES or NO answer eg., "Is it next to the post office?", "Was it at the start of our walk?" or "Is it nearer than the supermarket?".

assessment

Number:
Estimation
Shape and space:
Use mathematical terms to describe common 2D and 3D objects. Follow instructions related to movement and position.

Algebra:
Explore number patterns.
Handling data:
Use diagrams to represent a result of classification using one and two different criteria.

cross-curricular links

Geography:
Sketch their model from above and compare with the map or possibly an aerial photograph. Follow directions including the terms; forwards, backwards, up, down, left, right, North, South, East, West. Make a map of a short route showing features in the correct order.

investigation

Can you get to school without turning right?
Show me how you do this.

3   exploring our school

Take the children around the school. Ask them to record on A4 sheets of paper:
★   Something old
★   Something new
★   Any features which show symmetry
★   Any features which show cylinders, cones, triangles
★   Some right angles
★   Something beautiful
★   Something not nice
★   An interesting shape (s)
★   A tile pattern

This material can be used in the classroom to sort and identify all the various items found in the building, the shapes of all the special features and for aesthetic awareness. The children can decide how they display their work on the walls or make their own individual or group books.

Additional work could include:
★   Making a model of the school. They can draw views of their models from different positions including above if possible. These drawings can be compared with architects' drawings of the building if available.
★   Drawing a plan of the school. A challenging activity for some children would be to make the plan to scale.
★   Programming a Roamer or similar computerized toy to act as a post van to deliver messages around the school.
★   Using Logo to draw a view of the school with as much detail as the children can manage, using appropriate procedures for repeated features such as windows.
★   Looking at the school records so that they can find out for how many children the school was built. Making a graph which shows the number of children in the school every year from when it was built. Predicting the number of children likely to be on roll next year.

assessment

Number:
Estimation.
Shape and Space:
Use mathematical terms to describe 2D and 3D objects. Follow instructions related to movement and position.
Handling data:
Use diagrams to represent a result of classification using one and two criteria.

cross-curricular links

Geography:
Draw a plan view of a classroom.
History:
Find out the age of the building? What was on the site before? How many people were there? How has it changed?

investigation

Are most classrooms nearly square?
Show me how you know.

4   looking at walls, windows and interiors

walls
Take the children for a walk either around school or to a suitable nearby building in order to observe the patterns which are made by bricks. In school the children can:
★ Recreate these patterns using Lego bricks longwise and 'end on'.
Encourage the children to learn the names of the designs.
Record the brick patterns by potato or sponge printing etc.
★ Explore 'fault lines' in Lego walls. Talk to the children about the way that bricks in walls need to overlap each other in order to make the wall strong. A 'fault' line is created when the vertical joint in two or more rows (courses) of bricks is continuous. Having explored fault lines in Lego the children can investigate making different sized rectangles using '2' and '6' Cuisenaire rods. Neither vertical nor horizontal fault lines are allowed.
★ Explore making brick patterns by using a '1' Cuisenaire rod as a 'header' and a '3' rod as a 'stretcher'. The children can describe their pattern to their friend using words or numbers to indicate the connections, and interpret a digit pattern eg 1,3,1,3, by using the rods.

fault lines

windows

★ Encourage the children to note the number of panes in windows and the number of windows per house as they walk around the streets and roads. Back in school they can carry out calculations such as how many windows in the street, and explore the multiplication patterns produced by the window panes.

★ The children can draw and name the different shaped windows and window panes they saw on their walk.

interiors

Some buildings have very particular structures and uses. If you can arrange a visit to one it would certainly justify an in-depth study and provide an opportunity for the children to use their new-found knowledge and skills. Consider as possibilities — a place of worship, town hall, library, sports hall etc. Many of these places will have 'staff' who might be persuaded to add a commentary or answer questions. The children can follow as many as are feasible of the activities described in 'Exploring our school'. There should also be discussion about the materials used for the building. Arising from their observations ask the children to:

★ Design a plan for a room which has no right angles on 2 cm squared paper.

★ To use geoboards and elastic bands to show the plan of a house with only three right angles.

home/school link

Ask the children to draw the front and the back of their homes trying hard to indicate the detail of the features and the textures of the materials from which their home is built. (It is a common characteristic that both adults and children tend to define things by their outline and show small regard for the surface detail and texture.) In school their drawings can be sorted according to building material and a frieze can be made using the children's drawings. The shapes of the doors, windows and any embellishments can be discussed.

assessment

Number:
Calculate.
Algebra:
Explore number patterns.
Algebra:
Devise repeating patterns.
Shape and Space:
Recognise right angle corners.
Design using simple 3D tessellations.

cross-curricular links

Art/Craft:
Design and make a symmetrical stained glass window. Design a kneeler.
Geography:
Investigate where common materials are found. Observe and talk about a familiar place. Recognise that buildings are used for different purposes.
Science:
Collect other materials used for making buildings. The collection can be displayed and the children can make the labels. Consider whether materials used in buildings are natural or manufactured.

investigation

Most walls are made of identical bricks.
Can bricks be any shape?
Show me how you know.

5   looking at machinery & gadgets

Take another walk around your immediate locality, including a building site or road works if possible. Look for fixed pieces of equipment which help us in our daily lives (phone boxes, traffic lights, sign posts, cranes, etc) and note their locations.

On returning to school these items may be added to the model of the area made earlier. Discuss the USES of the items (to increase safety, to stop us from getting lost, to make jobs easier/quicker etc).

Discuss their PLACING. (Who put them there? Why were they there? Would they have been like that 'in the olden days'?)

If appropriate to your experience on the walk think about the scaffolding and encourage descriptions which clarify ideas about vertical, horizontal, angles, triangles, relating these especially to ladders leaning against walls .(What would happen if the foot of the ladder was a long way from the wall? Very close to the wall?) The children can experiment with strips of wood or rulers.

home-school link

Look for and record gadgets which are used in the home. (Cooking, household, garden and DIY.) In school make small picture cards of all the gadgets from the walk and home and sort them using one (Y1) or two (Y2) criteria (eg. use electricity, use muscle power, contribute to safety etc.) recording them in a variety of forms (Carroll, Venn, Tree diagrams etc).

guess which gadget

Using the set of cards, above, the children can play "I'm thinking about a ...." with one child holding a mental image of an object, which the others seek to identify by asking YES/NO questions. These questions and answers could be converted onto the BRANCH program and used as an identification tree.

climbing safely

The children can build some scaffolding using sticks, Meccano, Jinx etc and answer questions about the performance and construction of their structures using the correct vocabulary. They might also produce a parts list identifying the number of vertical, horizontal and sloping pieces used. This activity could be part of a technology problem solving exercise.

cogwheels

The children can assemble a collection of items (or photographs of items) which use cogwheels (egg whisks, drills, watches, clocks etc), and investigate their functioning. Using sets of cogwheels, they can play at linking them together and observing the direction in which they rotate and also the relative speeds of the different wheels. The children can play at being human cogwheels by linking arms, forming two circles and moving around one 'tooth' at a time. Can they manage three or four circles rotating together? What happens if there are twice as many people in one circle as in the other?

assessment

Shape and space:
Recognise right angles and compare with other angles.
Recognise rotation.
Use the terms clockwise and anticlockwise.

Handling data:
Use diagrams to represent the result of sorting and/or classifying using one or two criteria.

cross-curricular links

Art:
Make observational and imaginative drawings based on machines, and parts of machines.

Geography:
Explore the purpose, location and design of features in the local environment, for example traffic lights, crossings and post boxes.

Music:
Create a piece of music inspired by the noises of machinery, in a factory, kitchen or on a building site.

Science:
Investigate stability and rigidity in structures.

Technology:
Design a crane to move an object from A to B. Develop the idea of cogwheels to make something work using construction kits.

investigations

When there are a number of cogwheels does the last one go around in the same direction as the first?
Show me how you know.

6   looking at the food we eat

The children could draw individual pictures of the items they had for lunch. Discuss the origins of the food back to it's natural state, following through any manufacturing, packaging and retailing. A diagrammatic record could be made showing the stages involved in the production of a meal.

home/school link

Ask the children to record in picture form, the family meal.

In school:
★   Find out where each ingredient was obtained.
★   Add pictures of the items used in the home meal to the sorting done previously.
★   Establish foods that are 'natural' when bought, and others which have undergone a manufacturing process such as fish/fish fingers, potatoes/crisps.

workers
Make a list of all the people who are involved from start to finish in getting the meal on the table. Sort into 'people who make things', 'people who help us'... This list can be extended by adding the names of say, three people each child knows who is in paid employment.

waste
There can be much useful discussion with the children about litter around the school and in the classroom. Talk to the children about:
★   Is litter nice to look at?
★   Can it hurt wildlife?
★   Is it dangerous if we fall over it?

Create a chart to show the rest of the school what sort of litter is left around. Ask the children for help in deciding how to deal with the problem if there is one.

home/school link

The children can make a list or drawing of everything that is thrown away at the end of a meal. In school there could be discussion about:
★   What sort of things do we throw away?
★   Is it all necessary?
★   How much space does it take up?
★   Where does it all go?

★   Are dumps healthy places?
★   Look at the ways that children can help by recycling, buying in bio-degradable packages etc, re-using things instead of throwing them away?
★   Five or more things to do with an egg box before it is thrown away.

packaging

The children can make a collection of the packaging their food comes in. This can be sorted in various ways, 'material used', 'bio-degradable', 'stackability', 'colour', 'labelling', 'shape' etc. Possible investigations into packaging are many and numerous:

★   The concept of nets can be developed, first by experimenting with the given boxes/containers and then by designing the net of a container for a specific purpose eg., to carry three gingerbread people or other biscuits.

★   The idea of recycling can be further developed once it has been established that some packaging is made from aluminium and that aluminium is not attracted to magnets.

assessment

Shape and space:
Use mathematical terms to describe 3D shapes.
Construct simple nets.
Handling data:
Sort by 1 and 2 decisions.
Collect, record and interpret data.

cross-curricular links

Education for Economic & Industrial Understanding:
Trace a product from producer to consumer.
History:
Ask an older person to come into school to talk about shopping and cooking in their youth.

Science:
Consider similarities and differences in a variety of everyday packaging materials. Explore the properties of materials and see how some may be changed by simple processes such as bending, twisting, squashing etc. Investigate the extent to which a selection of everyday waste products decay naturally or can be recycled.

investigations

How many different nets will make an open cube box?
Show me.

7   exploring industry and waste through what we wear

sorting and examining

The children can sort materials as natural/man-made by reference to the manufacturer's labels. Explain the mixtures of the different materials eg. 60% nylon, 40% wool could be shown by 6 cups of water and 4 cups of water coloured blue. The children can see how many garments are natural fibre and how many are man-made fibre. The data can be represented by a pictogram or a bar chart. Talk about the differences there are between clothes made at home and clothes made in a factory.

a mini factory production line

Set up a mini factory production line. Talk about the fact that each person on a production line has his/her own particular job as part of the making process. A production line is created when 'lots' of identical items are needed. Let us consider that the children have decided that they would like to make for each child in the class a paper 'dressing up' doll's set, that is a cardboard figure with several paper outfits to 'dress' the body.

The set would contain:
★   A standard cardboard figure outline
★   A winter outfit eg. jeans and sweater
★   A summer outfit eg. T-shirt and shorts

Stencils would need to be made of the doll, the separate items of clothes to be used as patterns and the packaging envelope. Each child can submit a design for the prototypes. This could be turned into a competition if thought appropriate.

the production line

Identify the 'stations' of the production line: that is the separate stages necessary which might be:
★   Draw the body outline
★   Cut out the body outline
★   Draw in the facial features
★   Colour the hair
★   Draw the jeans
★   Draw the sweater

- ★ Draw the T-shirt
- ★ Draw the shorts
- ★ Colour/pattern the last four items separately
- ★ Cut out the clothes separately
- ★ Make an envelope for packaging
- ★ Label each packet
- ★ Package one of each item for future owner

manning the stations

There are 19 tasks. The tables for each 'station' should be suitably arranged around the room. Some 'stations' will need more time than others eg. cutting out the body outline will take longer than drawing the outline of the T-shirt, so it has to be decided whether one, two or three people are needed at that 'station'. The children can estimate – or better still time – each activity beforehand and decide on the number of children required. Each station must be 'manned' and resourced.

There may be the need for a 'resource' person so that each 'station' can call for more resources when they see their stocks running low.

training

The children will need to receive 'training' before they begin the real thing. This could be done by the people whose designs are being used. Consideration can also be given to being economical with the resources, that is, as many T-shirts as possible should be cut from each piece of paper so that paper is not wasted.

post production

The timing at each 'station' should be discussed; also the rate of production for each person and the sequence of events. This system could be adapted on other occasions to produce sweets, biscuits, masks for a school production etc.

home/school link

Make a list or picture of what you wear at other times of the year and clothes for specific activities (swimming, playing games, dancing, gymnastics etc). In school the most popular type of clothing can be identified through datahandling activities.

assessment

Length:
Compare measurements.
Time:
Measure intervals of time.
Handling data:
Sort using one or two criteria.

cross-curricular links

PSD:
Discuss clothes you don't wear any more. Are they worn out? Have you grown out of them? What will happen to them ? What could happen to them?
Geography:
Investigate garment labels identifying country of manufacture.

Science:
Consider different characteristics of materials used for clothing — appearance, feel, warmth, thickness etc. Look at the sources of fabrics and the different use made of them.

Technology:
Invent a production line for an item of classroom furniture.

investigation

My dad says…

How many stations would you need to mass produce Lego buggies to your design? Show me your plans.

CLIMATE

introduction

Climate is 'the long term prevalent weather conditions of an area, determined by latitude, position relative to oceans or continents, altitude etc'. Before they can begin to acquire a concept of 'climate', children must learn something of its chief 'building block', that is weather.

Weather is the 'day to day meteorological conditions, especially temperature, cloudiness and rainfall, affecting a specific place'.

The activities in this section are intended to increase children's experience of the accessible aspects of weather, and increase their awareness of how and why it has such an impact on their lives. From observing, feeling, and recording, the children will be encouraged to make predictions and find patterns in the weather. Although not strictly 'weather', investigation of the apparent movement of the Sun and Moon are included in this section.

discussion points

When does it rain?
Where does rain come from?
How does the sun shine?
When does the sun shine most?
Is it only hot when the sun is shining?
Is there 'weather 'at night?
When it's snowing here, is it snowing everywhere?
What is fog?
How do we get a shadow?
Does it always feel colder in the shade?

climate and weather

1   **Exploring** the weather
2   **Observing** the weather
3   **Recording** the weather
4   **Measuring** the weather
5   **Forecasting** the weather

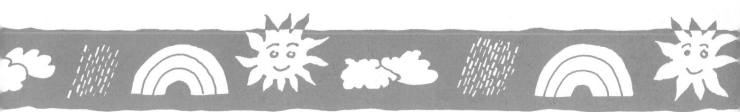

information

Investigating weather is just the first step towards an appreciation of the importance of climate. Children need to gain an awareness, experience and understanding of the elements of weather; record the presence or absence of patterns in each element and in the elements collectively; realise a place has a characteristic climate and that not all places have the same climate.

They need to appreciate that 'way of life' is strongly influenced by climate, partly due to the effect climate has on vegetation and hence on agriculture.

They also need to appreciate that, in addition to climate affecting people, people can also have an effect on climate, though not control it to any great extent.

Weather and climate are mentioned in both the Science and Geography National Curriculum documents. These refer to seasonal and daily changes, patterns in the changes, and the powerful effect weather has on people's lives. Children should be able to record and later measure temperature, rainfall, wind speed and direction. They should know why night occurs, that day length changes as does the inclination of the sun.

1   exploring the weather

Children should have opportunities to experience as great a variety of weather types as possible relative to the location of their school. They should show and talk about the out-door clothing they have worn to school; then, suitably dressed, they should be taken outside in all weathers to feel it, hear it and to play in it.

The children should go outside in:
★   Strong winds and light breezes – What does it feel like? Is there any sound? They should face the wind and then turn round to feel it on their backs.
★   Drizzle and heavy rain — (Shelter under a large (golf) umbrella or a tin roof.) Do they feel the same? Do they both make the same wetness? Do they sound the same? Do they both make puddles? Do they both make the same patterns in puddles? (Since these cannot be experienced at the same time, the children should be encouraged to describe, remember and recall.)
★   Hot and cold weather — What do they feel like? Do you feel hot all over, or do some parts of you feel hotter or colder than the rest?
★   Sunny and cloudy weather — Do you feel hot? Do you feel cold? What do you feel on a sunny winter's day? Do you feel hot on a cloudy day?
★   Wet and windy weather — Which is worst, the wet or the wind?
★   Snow, hail and fog — Can you hear snow/hail falling? What does it feel like?

The children should carry out 'play' or games activities in different weathers.
★   On a windy day, drop a feather/crisp packet and try to catch it — which way did it go? How did it move? How easily could you catch it? They should repeat this when there is a slight breeze. This activity could be recalled at a later time when the children are trying to measure wind strength.
★   Make a (seaside type) windmill, walk around outside with it on a windy day — when does it work best? Can you find a place where it won't work as well/at all? Do this on

a still, calm day — does the windmill work? Can you make it work? (by running and making it move through the air rather than the air move through it? Leading to the idea that WIND IS MOVING AIR).

★ Try to throw or catch a ball, and skip with a rope, into and against strong wind — what happens to the ball? Can you skip?

★ On a sunny day, try to lose your shadow, or catch another child's shadow — can you do it when someone is standing on your shadow?

★ When snow is on the ground, follow people's tracks — where did they go?

assessment

Temperature:
Compare hotness, windiness using appropriate language.

cross-curricular links

English:
Use the language opportunities for talking about their exploration of weather, and clothing appropriate for different types of weather, eg make up a story in the form of a newspaper article about chasing a feather in the wind, or tracking something or someone in the snow.

Music:
Make sound pictures or music about the rain on a roof or umbrella. Find a way of recording their music so that someone else can play it.

Geography:
Investigate the effects of weather on themselves and their surroundings.

Science:
Extend awareness of the variety of weather conditions and describe the changes in the weather. Choose the best material for a raincoat.

investigation

2 observing the weather

Remember the warning in the Science document of the National Curriculum: **NEVER LOOK DIRECTLY AT THE SUN.**

Throughout the activities in this section full use should be made of any information children have about children in other lands, especially in multi-ethnic schools and schools where children have experience of holidays abroad.

is the weather the same everywhere ?
Make a collection of clothes, or photographs of clothes, for all types of weather — in different seasons — in various parts of the world.
★   The children can sort them and explain their criteria for sorting eg., How they can tell the sun would be shining.   Why they think that it would be cold etc.

how do we dress for the weather ?
Make a collection of clothes for all seasons, (male and female) — possibly dolls clothes for these activities:
★   The children can sort out the clothes and dress dolls in the clothes appropriate for the weather of the day.
★   They can compare their ideas, and the clothes for the dolls with the clothes that they wear themselves. Do any of them match?
★   They can sort themselves according to the clothes they are wearing and explain their criteria for sorting.

will we go out to play ?
The children should discuss the weather in the morning and be asked:
★   Whether they think that it will change.
★   Whether they think that they will be able to go out to play in the morning, at lunch time and in the afternoon.
★   What chances are there of the children being right?
★   On what ideas were the children basing their predictions?
★   Can the children improve on today's predictions? The teacher can act as recorder or scribe and the children check and analyse their predictions.

are there patterns in the weather ?

home/school link

The children can ask five people if and when they went on holiday. The answers can be entered on a matrix. Replies can be collated back in school. Patterns can be sought on a variety of scales linking with the ideas used in the two previous paragraphs, and by adding discussion about birthdays and holidays.

★   **Annual:** make a time line to develop the relationship between summer holidays and sunshine, and winter holidays and snow (if appropriate to the school).

★   **Daily:** the children may recognise a link for example between dark clouds and rainfall, or sun, rain and rainbows, wind from one particular direction and cold weather.

Encourage the children to suggest and test ideas for patterns.

when jack frost is about

Encourage the children to identify a pattern for when 'Jack Frost' is about.

★ What is the time of year, time of day?
★ Is it hot or cold?
★ Is the sky clear or cloudy?
★ When does the frost go?
★ Is there a pattern to the weather which follows frost?
★ Can the children predict when it will be frosty/when there will be a frost overnight?
★ Where does it melt/disappear first, and why?
★ Where does it stay the longest and why? (relates to shadows)
★ Where does the frost come from and go to? The children can observe the patterns made by frost, on trees and branches, on the ground, on the windows.

assessment

Probability:
Make and test predictions.

cross-curricular links

Art:
Design and make, shadow puppets, designs for weather symbols, frost patterns or patterns based on observations of rain in puddles.

Drama:
Invent weather conditions and an appropriate lifestyle on another planet. Illustrate emotional reactions to different weather conditions.

Technology:
Design and make dolls' clothes choosing the most suitable materials for different types of weather.

investigation

Do most people take their holidays when it is hot?
Tell me how you know

3   recording the weather

the sun

inside the classroom

Use a classroom or school hall where the sun shines directly through the window. Discuss with the children whether having the sun shining directly in, inconveniences any child. Do they like the sun shining in their faces? To formalise their observations the children may:

★   Record the position of the sunshine by drawing around the shapes it makes on the floor and tables with chalk.

★   Draw a plan of the classroom and mark the plan at appropriate intervals during the day (every hour?), where the sun is shining in the room. A photocopy of the children's plan can be used by other children at other times.

★   Discuss their findings with the teacher.

outside the classroom

Remember to warn the children about not looking directly at the sun. Ask the children to go into the playground and stand at a point where they can look in the direction of the sun. Record their location and the direction of the sun. From their observations the children may be able to predict from which direction they will see the sun in an hour's time. Repeat the activity every hour and ask the children to explain their observations.

in the playground

The children will have noticed shadows at certain places around the school. Ask the children to record the position of the shadows at different times of the day. Again, see if they can explain their recording. Younger children could mark with chalk the position of the shadow produced by the school building or other appropriate features in the school grounds, such as football posts or trees.

a sundial

Now that the children should realise that the position of the sun is not constant, they are ready to be introduced to a sundial and use it for 'telling the time'.

Once the children have had experience of the movement of the sun and the relationship between this and the position of shadows, they may be able to consider the 'best location' for a sundial, a garden seat to sit on at playtime or a place to 'sunbathe'. This could be extended and could also be used, in the context of PLANTS AND ANIMALS, for the best location to plant a tree or a shrub, to put a new plant tub or several tubs to make a garden, or for the school pond etc.

the moon

home/school link

This activity develops further the idea of looking for patterns, and is better carried out in winter when it can be achieved at a reasonable hour in the evening. Ask the children to look at the moon each evening through the same window and note its position. They should also note its direction in relation to their home. In school they should then be asked to consider the assembled data, collected over more than a month and see if they can recognise a pattern.

the daily weather

The children may record the weather over a period of time using a matrix and a block graph. The children can decide whether they use words or pictures etc. The two should be compared.

assessment

Handling data:
Collect, record and interpret data.
Shape and Space:
Use language related to movement and position.
Time:
Use standard units of time.

cross-curricular links

Science:
Explore light sources other than the sun and their effect relating to shadows.
Observe changes in weather and relate them to the passage of time.

investigation

Does it gets colder when it rains?
Tell me how you found out.

4 measuring the weather

measuring windspeed and direction

Children will already have observed that the wind makes things move. They should use these observations to devise their own ways of measuring both the strength and the direction of the wind. The children could:

★ Make a list of the things they have noticed in their environment that move in the wind, eg. litter, trees, flags, smoke and washing.

★ Sort the list into 'things that do/do not indicate the direction in which the wind is blowing.'

★ Use the sorting to devise a way of measuring the wind direction, initially using their own method and terminology to indicate direction and then using the standard definition of N,S,E and W.

★ Sort the list into 'things that do/do not indicate the strength of the wind', initially using their own terminology to indicate strength. Those children ready for the standard measure of the Beaufort scale can be introduced to it here. (Some ideas are indicated in the 'Exploring Weather' section.)

★ Discuss the relationship between wind strength and wind speed since some of their ideas might be related to measuring strength and others to measuring speed, depending on whether or not the moving thing is fixed (eg branches on a tree) or free (eg litter).

★ Look for any things that indicate both strength and direction? Ask the children if they can measure the wind's strength and direction at the same time.

more measuring speed and direction

The children could design, make and use their own 'machine' for measuring the strength, speed or direction of the wind, or a combination of these.

recording wind speed and direction

When the children have devised ways of measuring wind speed, strength and/or direction they should record their measurements on a variety of time scales, (hourly, daily,) and present/communicate their data in their own way. They could then use rose diagrams or radial block graphs.

These activities may present an opportunity to introduce notions of angle, shadows, direction, height and width.

measuring shadows

The children will have already observed shadows around their school. In this activity the children will be using themselves to create a shadow. The children could work in pairs and:

★ Select an appropriate place to stand to get a good shadow, and record the location of the spot by any means they choose. They should discuss why they think that this is a good spot.

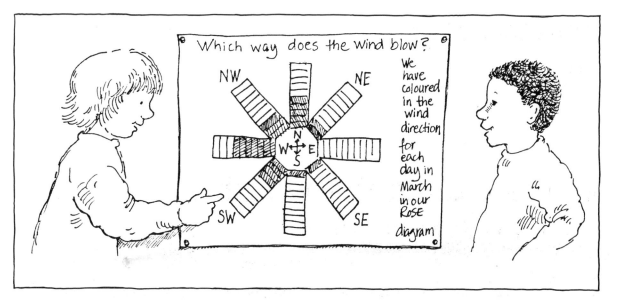

★ Measure the length and width of each others' shadow, and record the location at regular time intervals during the day. (They should talk about why they have chosen their intervals and how they know when it is time to measure again.)

★ Compare the measurements of their shadow with their own measurements to see if the shadow is the same size as they are. Are the length and the width the same? (They should be able to explain their discoveries.)

★ Repeat this activity using the shadow created by, for example, a tree.

★ Devise a way of measuring the height of the tree to compare the length of its shadow and record using their own methods.

measuring snow

Some schools will have more opportunities to carry out this activity than others! It is included here because it contains important safety points for children ie about snow drifts. After the children have had opportunities to watch the snow falling and settling, and to play in it, ask them to observe some snow which remains undisturbed. The children can be asked to :

★ Talk about the surface of the snow, looking in particular to see if it seems to be level, smooth, horizontal and the same shape of the ground underneath.

★ Look carefully at the snow to see if they can determine where they think that the snow might be deeper/shallower.

★ Devise a way of measuring its depth so that they can check their predictions.

★ Explain why more snow got to the deepest parts. (If the children have already done some work on wind they may be able to make connections.)

assessment

Length:
Use standard units for measuring.
Shape and Space:
Understand North, South, East and West.
Use language related to movement and position.

cross-curricular links

Geography:
Recognise seasonal weather patterns.
Describe weather patterns in different parts of the world.

Technology:
Design, make, and use a sundial.
Design, make and use an anemometer.
Design, make and use a depth gauge for measuring snow.

investigation

When are shadows shortest?
Tell me how you know.

5   forecasting the weather

Talk to the children about why people try to forecast the weather. The children can make a list of all the people who need/like to know what the weather is going to be tomorrow, at the weekend or next week.

the professional forecasters
The children might like to:
★   Record TV and radio weather forecasts, and collect newspaper forecasts.
★   Compare the forecasts from different sources to see if they all forecast the same sort of weather.
★   Compare the different forecasts with the actual weather to see if one of the sources is more accurate than the others.

children as weather forecasters
Ask the children if they have noticed any patterns in the weather. The children should be encouraged to:
★   Observe the clouds and record the associated weather over several days to see if there is any pattern.
★   Be aware of sudden changes in the weather, for example, when it suddenly goes dark during the day. Ask the children if they know what this indicates.
★   Devise ways of telling what the weather is going to be like this afternoon, tonight, tomorrow and to check their predictions, trying to determine the most reliable indicators of the weather. The children should devise their own ways of recording, checking and communicating the various forecasts.

home/school link

Ask the children to make a collection of weather rhymes. They may find that their grand parents are particularly helpful. There are lots of them often involving plants and animals, especially birds. They may like to make up their own sayings from the observations. The most obvious relationships can usually be made with reference to clouds; their colour, shape and height in the sky. In school the children could test the rhymes for accuracy and find out which is the most reliable rhyme.

The children could find out:
★   If a red sky in the morning indicates 'shepherd's warning'.
★   If the ash is out before the oak does it mean that there will be a wet summer?

- ★ Does seaweed forecast the weather accurately?
- ★ What changes to the weather does the barometer record? Even though they do not understand about a barometer the children can see if the 'rising' or 'falling' does indicate the changes accurately.
- ★ The most reliable rhyme.

assessment

Handling Data:
Collect, record and interpret data.
Make and check predictions.
Recognise that outcomes can vary.

cross/curricular links

English: Present own weather forecast as a TV weather person.
Present own weather forecast as a radio weather person.
Compare the two exercises.

investigation

Neela says...

Are weather forecasts always right? Tell me how you know.

ENERGY

introduction

This theme is predominantly a science one. As with almost all scientific work every activity involves much mathematics both in using measuring instruments and in the handling of data. For young children, especially with such an advanced and complex concept as 'energy', it is essential to start with what they know and can experience and to look at the evidence they see associated with the word 'energy'. This experience is usually the result of energy being used in the form of heat, light, sound or movement.

It is assumed, in this theme, that 'Energy' has been introduced in the usual way - in Science, Health care, technology etc. This book is about mathematics in the environment. Under this heading, with young children, the environment has to include the children themselves and the toys they play with.

We consider the claims and sayings that they hear in their daily lives and the experiences they have every day at home, in school and on the way to school.

discussion points

ourselves
Why do we go to bed? Could we walk for ever? What would happen if you watched T.V. all day and all night? How do you feel after running around the playground lots of times? What would you do to recover? Does anyone ever say to you "You're full of energy today"? What do they mean? Where do you get your energy?

animals
Do animals get tired? Do they run around a lot? Do you think that a hamster needs the same amount of energy as you? Does it need as much as a lion? Where do animals get their energy?

machines and things
What makes a machine work? Where does electricity come from? What makes a toy car with no engine move? Where does it get its energy? What do these machines do? (Pick out machines and things which give light, give out heat, have a cooling effect, make a noise or move.)

energy

resources

40

A set of toys which are powered in a variety of ways (water, clockwork, elastic bands etc.)

information

We need carbohydrates and fats in our food to give us energy. This type of food can only be made by green plants; therefore we need either to eat plants, or animals which have eaten plants. The plants need carbon dioxide, water and minerals as the ingredients for making this food (they are not the food). The plants turn these ingredients into food using energy in the form of light. Proteins are basically for growth and repair and contain very little energy. (In starvation situations they would be used for energy.)

1 playing with energy

toys

The children can make a collection of toys from home and school which use a variety of energy sources. The collection should include toys which are water powered, battery operated, clockwork or use elastic bands.

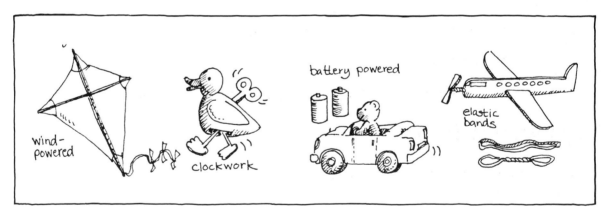

As the children play with the toys discussion can centre on questions such as:
★   Where is this toy getting it's energy?
★   Why has it stopped?
★   Which toy goes the greatest distance?
★   Which toy keeps going the longest?
★   Which toys run in a circle?
★   Which toys move in a straight line?

ourselves

A. Talk to the children about their favourite games and pose questions such as:
★ Which do they like best?
★ What do they play in the playground?
★ Do they like ball games?
★ Which games do they like watching on TV?
★ Which games make the children feel tired?
★ What sort of game do the children play which does not make them feel tired?

B. Take the children outside and get them to cover a given distance, say 50m, in different ways such as running, skipping, hopping and jumping with feet together. Ask the questions:
★ Which activity takes up the most energy?
★ Which activity takes up the least?
Back in the classroom the children can draw pictures of themselves doing the different activities, and then attempt to put the drawings in 'energy level' order.

assessment

Length:
Direct comparison.
Time:
Direct comparison.
Handling data:
Ordering data.
Shape and Space:
Use mathematical terms to describe common 2D shapes.

cross-curricular links

Art/English:
Explain either graphically, orally or by writing how they feel after these exercises.
PE:
Compare exercises and games for their energy requirements.
Explore different ways of moving around to 'save' energy.
Science:
Discuss how children get their energy.
Technology:
Design and make vehicles for transporting friends using large scale construction kits.

investigation

Can clockwork toys travel in straight lines better than battery operated toys?
How do you know?

2 observing energy

Establish in discussions with the children that some things, for instance machines, do not work on their own. They need to be switched on or be wound up. These items also have a function. They can be used to keep people warm, keep things cold, give us light, make noises, clean and move.

The children can make collections of pictures of the above items and sort them. As the pictures are sorted there will be opportunities to discuss the sources of energy which make the machines/equipment work:

eg   Fire   - coal, gas, electricity, paraffin, oil, wood
         Calculator   - battery, sunshine (light)
         Piano   - person's fingers
         Bicycle   - person's legs

Other sources will be petrol, wind, solar, nuclear, gravity etc.

home/school link

The children can look around their homes and list and draw machines and other things indicating their sources of energy. In school they can use these lists to make bar charts or block graphs such as:
- ★   This block graph shows what makes our fires hot at home.
- ★   A bar chart to show how many people have battery or solar powered calculators.

Discussion can be centred around the implications of the findings - for instance there may not be a gas main in the village or there may be a local industry which provides coal or wood.

ourselves

The children can devise a recording system which will show how energetic they feel during the day. If they do not suggest any ways themselves ask them to use smiley or miserable faces.

They will need to record how they feel:
- ★   When they first wake up.
- ★   Just before breakfast.
- ★   After breakfast.

- ★ Before lunch.
- ★ After lunch.
- ★ At home time.
- ★ At bedtime.

If it can be arranged let the children wait an extra hour or so before having their midday meal one day. This could be linked to a charity appeal to help children realise what feeling hungry is like. (Obviously normal health considerations and individual children's needs must be considered.) Some schools have organised an appeal with older children, in which they give up a lunch and send the equivalent money to a charity appeal for famine relief. With young children they could be encouraged to go without their mid morning snack and give that cost to charity. In either situation an element of official or parental consent may be advisable.

assessment

Handling Data:
Sort a set of objects.
Handling data:
Interpret block graphs and frequency tables.
Number:
Use numbers in the context of the classroom and school.
Time:
Language associated with times of the day.

cross-curricular links

History:
Consider what life was like without electricity.
Consider mode of use for 'old-fashioned' artifacts such as flat irons.
PE/Drama:
Behave in different ways; fast, slow, full of energy, worn out etc.

investigation

My brother Marcus says...

Are children more energetic before or after lunch? Show me how you know.

4   conserving energy

Before starting this section it is necessary to establish that the children appreciate the sources of energy; underground (fossil fuels), overground (wood) or from the elements (sun, wind and water). They should realise that people have to work hard to get natural resources which are changed and transported to us. This work must be paid for so energy costs.

where does energy come from and who pays?

The children can be asked:
*   How are your meals cooked at home?
*   How is your home heated?
*   Where does the energy come from?
*   Do your parents have to pay for the energy you use in your house?
*   How does the gas/electric company know how to charge your parents for the energy used in your home?
*   Do you pay for your solid fuel/oil/paraffin?
*   Where does it come from?
*   How does it get into your home?
*   What does the school use for cooking, heating and lighting?
*   How do the suppliers know how to charge the school?

home/school link

The children can be shown the meters at school and asked to find, draw and label their meters at home and find out whether they have more than one meter. Those children who use other energy sources can draw the sources being brought into the home, whether it is coal being brought in by car or oil in a tanker. In school they can find out how much it costs. Up-to-date Unit costs will need to be obtained by the teacher from the relevant suppliers. Gas & Electricity Boards often produce information packs and leaflets. Most often this is aimed at older children but useful facts may be extracted.

The children can also find out:
*   How long are the classroom lights on each day?
*   How much does it cost to keep them on?
*   How much does it cost to watch my favourite TV programme?
*   How long can the cooker be on for a pound?

The unit costs may need to be 'rounded' for use by very young children unless they are confident with the decimal point and the calculator.

is there any 'free' energy?

The children can make a collection of items and pictures of machines which use 'free' energy. They will need to look for things which are powered by water, wind, and solar power. These pictures and objects can be sorted.

saving energy

*   The children may like to make a list of all the things they would be able to eat should there be no electricity at school for one day.
*   The children can consider what they would do should there be no electricity for lighting in winter.
*   The children can make a list of the things they could/could not do to reduce the amount of money spent by the school.

assessment

Number:
Solve problems involving multiplication.
Number:
Interpret a range of numbers in the context of measurement and money.
Handling Data:
Access information from a time table.
Time:
Measuring using standard units.

cross-curricular links

Science:
Experience simple activities using bulbs, buzzers, batteries and wires and investigate materials which do/do not conduct electricity.
Technology:
Design and make toys which use 'free' power — wind/elastic band.

investigation

Some manufacturers claim that their batteries last longer than anyone else's. Are they right? Are they better value for money? Explain your answer to me.

5 transferring energy

This section links very closely with technology. Whilst commercially produced toys may be useful, it is most desirable that the children have opportunities to make their own powered toys. The testing that becomes possible will depend upon the constructions produced and should become self-evident.

However, the following may serve as examples:

★ Measure distances travelled by different toys.
★ Measure distances travelled by different samples of the same toy.
★ Measure distances travelled against energy input eg 10 winds of elastic band compared with 20 winds.
★ Measure comparative strengths of children:
      - Pushing a toy
      - Blowing a ball
      - "Strong man hammer"
      - Squeezing a plastic bottle to force liquid up a tube.

Several tests for each exercise will provide more data for handling and also lead to more conclusive results.

assessment

Handling Data:
Interpret data which has been collected by pupils.
Length:
Compare lengths.
Measure lengths.

cross-curricular links

Science:
Experience toys which move and store energy.
Experience natural and manufactured forces which push, pull, move things, stop things and change the shape of objects.
Technology:
Experiment with and construct artifacts or systems using electrically powered motors.

investigation

PEOPLE AND THEIR COMMUNITIES

introduction

The activities in this section are intended to make children more aware of how they fit into the community; to recognise the similarities and differences between people in their community; to identify activities carried out by people in the local area; to describe ways in which people have changed their environment; to understand how they communicate, and to help them develop ideas about improving the environment in and around school.

discussion points

What is a family?
Has your family always lived here?
If not, why have they come here?
Can you find when they came here?
Do you know where they lived previously?
Do we live in a town, a village, a city?
Can children look after themselves?
Do people need other people in order to live?
How do we find out what's happening around us?

people and their communities

1   **Playing** at Families & Workers
2   **Exploring** families
3   **Looking** at ourselves
4   **Exploring** shopping
5   **Looking** at people who work in our community

information

There are many links between this section and **Buildings, Industrialisation and Waste**.

1 playing at families & workers

Key stage 1 children should have opportunities to explore and experience the different roles that people play in real life. It is through role play that they will begin to understand the complexities of what working involves, what people actually do and why they dress in certain ways. It is not always necessary to provide exact replicas of outfits, a multi-purpose set of overalls can be used one day as the waste disposal operator's dress and the next day a painter's. Quite frequently hats will turn something general into a specific outfit: Areas in the classroom can be turned into shops, factories or schools with few props but a lot of imagination. These free play situations will produce much mathematical language.

making an environment

Using Small World people, junk, Plasticine and bricks children can make their own small communities in sand trays filled with compost or sand. Before the children start building their environments talk with them about the various things they can use and areas which might have a specific character such as:

★   A seaside town
★   A housing estate with a play area
★   A shopping mall
★   A market
★   A village
★   A farm

Before they start modelling, see if the children can design/plan or draw a picture of what they think that their environment will look like.

After the activity discuss the drawing/model and the reality of the play situation:
★   Did they match?
★   Why?
★   Would they like to live there?
★   What would improve it?

There also need to be questions which will stretch the children's mathematical ideas and vocabulary, particularly with reference to notions of size and scale, such as:

★ Is your field big enough for more than one horse?
★ Can your play people fit in the houses?
★ Are your swings far enough away from the activities so that they do not create dangers for other children?

playing at shopping

A "NEW TOWN" DESIGN (Based on an original idea by Wendy Lankester)

Let the children form themselves into friendship groups and invent a family and a family name for themselves. They can have grandparents, mother and father and children or only parts of a family. Then they can choose what business or facility they would like to provide for the New Town in which they live. They may need help in choosing. Here are a few examples to start them thinking: Post Office, newsagents, bank, dance studio, school, public house, bus service, hospital (try your local hospital to see if they lend sets of miniature clothing) etc. There should be lots of discussion about the importance of each person's job and their contribution to the overall scheme.

Identify areas for each group to set up their business, and ask the children to collect items for them and for their special clothing. Once all the families have established their businesses a special occasion can be set aside for the Town to be brought to life. At the chosen time give the children time to set up their areas then divide the class into two groups. One group will need to put CLOSED signs on their doors because there must be a population free to experience the facilities on offer. Alternatively it may be possible to invite the pupils from another class to be the customers and consumers. Money to 'spend' in the village can be obtained by the children from a bank or post office using pension books or cheque books. The totals involved will, of course, need to reflect the sums of money they are capable of handling. The children make their transactions and use their money to experience the delights of their new town. The discussions as the children move around, buying and selling, will promote good mathematics. Teachers will be free to check the purchases and bills of the children and to provide new pension or cheque books where necessary. Some children will be able to keep their own business accounts.

assessment

Money:
Use coins in simple contexts.
Solve whole number problems involving addition and subtraction using money.

cross-curricular links

Art:
Paint pictures (photographs) of the family.
English:
Invent and write up a family history.
Geography:
Talk about homes/businesses being part of a settlement and that settlements vary in size.
Talk about a familiar place.
Technology:
Design publicity material for enterprises.

investigation

Do most of the businesses in our new town sell food?
Show me what you found out.

2 exploring families

Children should be helped to feel good about their families and their cultures.

home/school link

Ask the children to put the names of their family in the 'bricks' of a drawing of a wall section. The children can go in the top row, parent(s) in the next and grandparent(s) in the bottom. In school these 'walls' can be displayed and, by making graphs, the children can find out the most frequently appearing names on each of the levels.

venn/carroll diagrams
The children can put pictures of themselves onto a Carroll or Venn diagram which sorts according to two criteria:
★   have a brother
★   have a sister
Then the children can draw their families. These pictures can be displayed in close proximity to the Carroll or Venn diagram.

school census
A survey can be made of all the children in the school recording their name, date of birth and also details of what they would like to do when they grow up. The pupils can decide the best way to record and display this material.

home census

The children can ask everyone in their house what paid work they do now and what other employment they have had. They can also ask other members of their families such as Grandparents and Aunts and Uncles what work they did/do. These occupations may be sorted by various categories and recorded on a time line indicated by the age of starting the job. In school the children can draw their relatives individually and label the picture with the occupation. These pictures can be sorted by various categories. The children can also put their information on a time line. This time line could indicate, for instance, that Mummy was a secretary in 1984 and a Dinner lady in 1991 etc. Discussion could demonstrate changes in employment patterns.

assessment

Money:
Read, write and order numbers to 2000.
Handling data:
Sort using two criteria.
Handling data:
Collect, create and interpret data.

cross-curricular links

English:
Collect popular playground songs from their family or members of the community. Record the songs sung in the playground at the present time and make notes of changes and variations.
Display old photographs of the school and the community, along with any vintage tools or artifacts that the older people may have in their homes, or which may be borrowed from secondhand shops or the local museum.
Geography:
Identify activities carried out by people in the local area.
Explain why some activities in the local area are located where they are.
Recognise that adults do different kinds of work.
History:
Talk to old people who live near the school about former occupations. Record these conversations on video tape or on a tape recorder.
Technology:
Design a display of photographs (see above).

investigation

Does everyone have just one job in their lives?
Tell me what you found out.

3   looking at ourselves

This section will make children aware that they have individual needs but these must be reconciled with those of society.

festivals

Make a calendar for a year and display the festivals and celebrations that are kept by each of the children in the class. In a mono-culture classroom the children can find out about other festivals and celebrations from books and from people who have been invited in from the community.

home/school link

The children can ask at home for dates and places of their birth, christening or comparable occasions: how old they were when they started school, how old they will be when they leave. This information can be shared and compared in the classroom on charts. They can find out how old children are when they start school in other countries.

other opportunities for handling data

Let the children decide the information they would like to acquire about their classmates. They can choose from:

★   Our favourite game.
★   Our favourite football team.
★   How far we travel to school.
★   Our Ethnic origin (include Irish, Welsh etc.)
★   How long each family has lived in the area.
★   Which county/country our grandparents live in.
★   Do we regularly visit a church or any other religious place with our parents? Describe the places visited.

These activities may run alongside or be used to extend the usual classroom topic about 'Ourselves.'

places used by our family

home/school link

The children can be asked to find out the places their family uses such as medical centres, baby clinics, Bingo halls, football stadia, schools etc. What do the grandparents use? How far do people have to travel to these places? In the classroom this information can be collated by the children.

assessment

Handling data:
Collect, record and interpret data.
Time:
Ordering events using a calendar.

cross-curricular links

Geography:
Recognise that buildings are used for different purposes.
Talk about the uses of homes, shops, offices, factories, schools, places of worship.
Describe ways in which people make journeys.

History:
Interview someone about differences between past and present schools, transport, shops and fashion.
Sequence events in children's own lives.

PSD:
Talk about the use of rules in society and school.

Technology:
Design clothing for a special purpose such as new kit for the football/netball team, personal festival party clothes or wedding clothes.

investigation

Bobbie says...

Does everything belong to someone?
Tell me how you found out.

4   exploring shopping

Shopping is an important feature of modern life. Everyone has to buy items from time to time. Children can learn the importance of commerce through questioning shop keepers and their family.

shopping

Ask each child to draw a picture of a shop they have visited recently or seen on their way into school in the morning. (Country children can draw a picture of the shop they last visited.) The pictures should be labelled where possible. Using a decision tree or other sorting diagram, the children can sort the pictures according to their own criteria. Can they justify their criteria? They may choose to sort in some of the following ways:

These shops:
★   Sell food/do not sell food
★   Sell clothes/do not sell clothes

* ★ Sell shoes/do not sell shoes
* ★ Sell fruit and vegetables/do not sell fruit and vegetables
* ★ Sell newspapers/do not sell newspapers

Quite soon the children will be able to determine the criteria by which they sort the shop pictures. Much discussion should follow, with the children perhaps arriving at a conclusion that not all shops have clearly defined ares of merchandise while other shops are still specialist.

probability

The children can make a set of pictures of goods they need or are needed in their lives eg. clothes and things which help to keep them clean and tidy (jumper, trousers, iron, soap powder, washing machines). Have three boxes which can be labelled either 'Certain' 'Impossible' or 'Maybe', or alternatively, 'Yes', 'No' or 'Maybe'. Place the three boxes in a row with a descriptive label eg. Electrical Shop.

Each child picks up a picture and asks the question, "Will I find this item in this shop?" and places the card in the correct box. At other times the labels could be changed to:

* ★ Green grocer
* ★ Supermarket
* ★ Butcher etc.

or a different set of pictures made.

visiting shops

The following activities can be carried out with a small group of children visiting one shop with an adult. Before the children visit the shop they should decide which questions they would like to have answered.
They could ask questions about the shop such as:

* ★ What do you sell?
* ★ What is the dearest/cheapest thing you sell?
* ★ Where do your goods come from?
* ★ How far do your goods travel?
* ★ What sort of transport do your goods arrive in?
* ★ What time of the day do your goods usually arrive?
* ★ What time do you open and close?
* ★ Has this always been a (butchers) shop?
* ★ Do you like your job?
* ★ What is the best thing about your job?
* ★ How long have you worked here?
* ★ Have you always worked in a shop?

Photographs may be taken of the shops for use in school.

From the data gathered the children can use decision trees, graphs and charts in order to find out these things:

* ★ The cheapest item in any shop.
* ★ Whether shopkeepers like their jobs.
* ★ How long the shopkeeper has been in his/her job.
* ★ Which countries export to the U.K?
* ★ Does any one country send only one kind of goods?
* ★ Which are the imported goods?

Other visits could be made to a supermarket, an open air market etc. with the children finding out similar information.

This work will fit in with the 'bread and butter' money maths which is part of Maths in the National Curriculum.

making a real shop

Famine and natural disasters such as floods and hurricanes are, sadly, all too often in the news. Children may wish to raise money in response to the needs of the people affected by such events, or to help with, for example, Blue Peter or 'guide dog' appeals. This decision may provide a practical opportunity for the children to experience the real world of finance.

The children will need to:

★   Decide what their stall, cafe or shop will sell and where it will be located.

★   Decide prices for their stock.

★   Decide the date, time, venue and potential customers.

★   Design and make the posters or invitations and organise their distribution.

★   Decide on the overheads such as cost of materials.

assessment

Number:

Solve problems using all four operations with money.

Handling data:

Sort, collect, record and interpret data.

Probability: Recognise that there is a degree of uncertainty about the outcome of some events but that others are certain or impossible.

cross-curricular links

Technology:

Draw from information about materials, people, markets and processes and from other times and cultures to help in developing their ideas.

investigation

If I give you 50p how many different ways could you spend it in your class shop?

Show me what you have found out.

5   looking at people who work in our community

inviting people into school

Talk to the children and ask them who they would like to come into school and talk to them about their work. The children can decide what questions they would like to ask and how they would record the information. They may need prompts about the sort of things they would like to find out.

Eg. For a shop assistant:

★ How long has s/he been in this job? ★ How many other jobs has s/he had? ★ Did her/his parents do this job? ★ How important does s/he feel that her/his job is? ★ How many hours a day does s/he work? ★ What sort of training did s/he have? ★ What else would s/he like to do? ★ At what age did s/he start work?

making a questionnaire

Following on from the above activity the children may see the need for a quicker way of finding out about people's work. They can decide in groups the questions and format of a questionnaire they will ask workers to fill in. This information will need to be fed into a proper computer database such as 'Data show' or 'Fact file'. Some children will need help from a grown-up, but it is especially important that every one has a chance to input data as well as interrogate it. The easiest questionnaires to work on are those which have Yes/No answers, multiple choice answers or answers which can be listed. With all questionnaires it is imperative to decide in advance what use will be made of the information and how it will be recorded/evaluated.

sorts of work

Provide the children with people to talk to and places to visit which will give the children information about the work that was historically available in the vicinity.

The type of work can be listed in three sections:

★   The primary section — 'Those people who work on or under the land or sea'.
★   The secondary section — 'People who make things'.
★   The tertiary section — 'People who help us'.

assessment

Handling data:
Sort, collect, record and interpret data.

cross-curricular links

Art and English:
Make a portrait gallery with pictures, photographs and descriptions of everyone who works in and for the community.
Geography:
Talk about people they have seen working and what they do.

investigation

PLANTS AND ANIMALS

introduction

Children will learn about plants and animals more generally in Science and in Geography. However, there are many occasions when plants and animals may be used to promote mathematical activities, particularly those involving collecting, sorting and data handling. This section looks at some of those opportunities and considers ways in which they may be used to good advantage.

The activities will encourage children to become aware of the great variety of both plants and animals in their home and school environments — as well as further afield, and to appreciate the conditions and treatment plants and animals need to flourish.

They will also help children to understand the dependence of animals on plants and of people on both plants and animals. Through all the work in this section there must be a strong emphasis on caring for plants and animals in their environment, especially encouraging children to be gentle with animals and not to pick flowers or damage plants, shrubs and trees. Whilst it has been convenient to talk about plants and animals separately, it is important that the children see the two as strongly inter-related and inter-dependent and have both in mind when they make their observations and conclusions. They also need to develop an understanding that humans are animals.

Children should have the opportunity to explore plants and animals through play both inside and outside the classroom. Children should be encouraged to explore the environment for plants and animals at all times of the year, not only in the summer when they are most abundant, so that they become aware of change.

They may need encouragement to explore the environment with patience, persistence and care, and to learn to watch quietly and be alert to the occasional visitors not normally noticed - scavenger birds in the playground after breaktimes and more timid birds which they might need to watch from a window.

Minibeasts will be present in all environments and in most settings larger animals and birds will also be found. From their experience children may have some ideas about where minibeasts might be found - in soil, dust, under stones, in walls (gently 'tickling' at the edges of a hole in a wall with a blade of grass will often bring forth a spider from his home!). They could also place objects at certain locations to see if they can attract animal life by providing suitable habitats. Whether the school environment is urban or rural there will be animal and plant life close to the school, although it may not always be easy to find.

discussion points

What is an animal?	What is a plant?
Do all animals have fur?	Do plants grow?
How many legs do animals have?	Do all plants have leaves/flowers
Are insects animals?	Are trees plants?
Why do people keep animals?	Why do people grow plants?
Are all animals tame?	Which parts of plants do we use/eat?
Which is the most popular pet?	Which is the most common tree near school?
Do all countries have the same animals?	Do all countries have the same plants?

plants and animals

1   **Exploring** plants and animals
2   **Visiting** plants and animals
3   **Observing** plants and animals
4   **Examining** plants and animals
5   **Using** an animal product
6   **Designing** a garden
7   **Plants and animals** as living things

resources

An outdoor pond might encourage spawning especially if a little spawn is introduced. Hopefully the resulting adults will 'adopt' the pond. A very limited amount of spawn could be introduced to an indoor pond (suitably aerated), but the froglets or toadlets should be returned to their 'home' pond at the appropriate time. Appropriate food plants (nettles and brassicas – cabbages – for instance) could be grown in a convenient spot to encourage butterflies and then their caterpillars.

1   exploring plants and animals

Depending on the location of the school the balance between indoor and outdoor work will vary, but whatever the location children always enjoy planting seeds and watching them grow. The familiar mustard and cress, beans, peas, bulbs and sunflowers are all reliable examples. Growing things outside in beds, tubs or 'growbags' widens the experience and avoids some of the watering and care problems associated with plants grown in the classroom.

As well as growing the usual seeds already mentioned, the children could also be given the opportunity to participate in these situations and answer these questions:

★   Grow herbs for their scent and taste. Can you recognise the different smells? Do some grow faster than others?

★   Plant a tree when they start school and make it 'their' tree to care for and chart its growth over the years. Is it the same all the year round? What happens to its leaves? How much do you think it will grow this year?

★   Take responsibility for pot plants in the classroom or corridor. How often do we need to water them? How much water do they need? Do they all need the same amount of water? How can we remember when to water them?

- ★ Be gardeners - using garden tools, digging raking, riddling, weeding etc. When do most weeds grow?
- ★ Observe the shrubs, hedgerows, trees along the roads and in parks and gardens noticing the differences between the wild and cultivated, the formal and the informal. Do some hedgerows have more bluebells/other wild flowers than others? What shapes do the shrubs remind you of?
- ★ Explore grassland. Is it all grass? How tall is the grass? What sound does it make in the wind?

Similar practices may be even more important with minibeasts and animals, as the children will often be less familiar with them and more apprehensive of their presence. The following are possibilities:

- ★ Caring for small animals and insects (minibeasts) including worms, woodlice, stick insects, caterpillars, snails and spiders will help children to overcome any fears and phobias they may have. They can be asked if the animals tickle when handled? Are they nice to stroke? Do they look the same? What are the differences between any of the minibeasts?
- ★ Consideration of the food that minibeasts and animals eat. Where does the food come from? Is the food plant or animal? Is it eaten raw or cooked? Which part of the plant is eaten? Do the plants grow in this country?
- ★ Since we are also animals - consider where our meat or fish comes from? Which plants do we eat?

assessment

Number:
Use numbers in the context of classroom and school. Make a sensible estimate of a number of objects.

cross-curricular links

Science:
Know that there is a wide variety of living things including mammals.

investigation

Vijay says...

If you ask an equal number of mums and dads would more mums or dads be afraid of spiders? Show me how you know.

2 visiting plants and animals

There are many places with plants and animals that children could visit. We most frequently visit parks, woods, farms and perhaps zoos but we could also go to market gardens, garden centres, fruit and vegetable markets, greengrocers shops or museums with animal collections. In many of these places there will be someone willing to explain things to the children.

Alternatively it may be possible to have animals brought into school from zoos, wildlife parks or animal collections.

Try to make it possible for children to:
★ Experience the size of animals - illustrations often fail to suggest size or scale. Is a sheep or kangaroo bigger or smaller than their dog? How tall is a horse or a penguin? Which is the smallest furry animal they can see?
★ See young animals and talk about ages and sizes. How big was it when it was born? At what age do different animals stop growing? How long do they stay with their mother?
★ See the sizes, shapes and colours of the fruits and vegetables on display at the greengrocers or in the supermarket. How are the apples and oranges arranged? Which fruit or vegetable would roll around easily? Which ones are nearly all the same size? Which are long and thin? Are all green fruits round?
★ See a wide variety of pot plants noticing similarities and differences in shape, size, colour, pattern, feel, smell. Are all the flowers open at the same time? Are all the same type of flower the same colour? Are all the plants in the same size pot?
★ Experience walking through a wood. Are all the tree trunks tall and straight? Are some trunks fat or thin? Compare some sizes using tape measure or string. Are all leaves the same shape? How many different leaves can you collect (from the ground)? How does it sound when you walk through the leaves? Listen to the sound of the wind in the trees. Listen for birds and animals.

assessment

Handling data:
Sort a set of objects describing criteria chosen.
Length:
Comparison.
Order by estimation of length.

cross-curricular links

Geography:
Make a representation of a real place, for example the distribution of trees and or flower beds in a park.

investigation

Can you tell by its shape whether a fruit or vegetable will roll in a straight line, along a curve or not roll at all?
How do you tell?

3   observing plants and animals

Observation of plants and animals may be carried out in their natural habitat. When it can be done without causing damage to the environment, it is sometimes convenient and interesting to bring collections of items into the classroom for more detailed and extensive study.

There are many opportunities throughout the year to make collections of plants and animals, and artefacts associated with them. Such collections can be used for all the usual sorting activities and the outcomes recorded in a variety of ways — either devised by the children or using the conventions of Carroll, Venn and Tree diagrams. Many of these activities, especially those with plants (eg leaves, fruits and berries), are well documented elsewhere and therefore not repeated here.

Collections could be built up continuously, but it will often be desirable to have regard for the seasons in assembling specific groups of items for display and consideration:

plants
★   **Autumn** - Harvest, fruits and berries, fallen leaves
★   **Spring** - Seeds, bulbs, buds
★   **Summer** - Leaves, flowers, growing things
★   **Winter** - Twigs, tree debris
Discussion can establish the cyclic nature of the seasons and the similarities and differences between the items in each collection.

communities of animals
Some 'collections' or communities of animals may be observed and enjoyed outdoors without unduly disturbing them. For minibeasts it may be possible to set up favourable environments which can be discreetly monitored over a period of time and facilitate longer studies of changes and populations. Those fairly readily available may include:
★   Snails - especially on walls behind climbing plants
★   Woodlice - under bricks stones and slabs
★   Ladybirds - on aphid infested plants, especially rose trees.

Daily records may be kept and displayed. The exercise will provide opportunities not only for counting the number present but also for making predictions. How many will there be tomorrow? Will there be as many/more/fewer next week? Do they stay in small groups, big groups or live alone?

Comparisons of different species may be made and the observations classified using a simple database. They might also record variations in size or count the ladybird's spots, for example.

caterpillars and spawn
Children usually find caterpillars fascinating. They are often adept at locating caterpillars and enjoy observing and recording a community of them, especially their changes in size and colour.

The observations could be recorded and illustrated on a time line. The cyclic nature of the life cycle can be represented using a circular recording format such as a hoop hanging from the ceiling.

Similarly the children might enjoy locating toad or frog spawn and observing and recording change. The observations could be related to a time line etc as with the caterpillars.

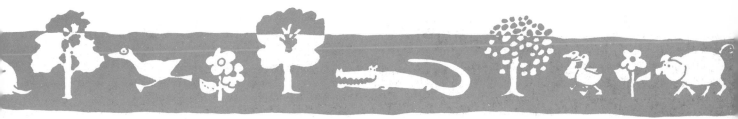

March 3	March 4	March 5	March 6	March 7	Mar
day 1	day 2	day 3	day 4	day 5	day
Today we found some frog spawn.	we cannot see any change.	There is still no change to see.	Little tadpoles are beginning to hatch.	Today there are more tadpoles.	Tod mor

assessment

Number:
Use numbers in the context of the classroom and school.
Make a sensible estimate of a number of objects.

cross-curricular links

Art\Craft:
Observe and draw plants and animals.
Geography:
Use a large scale map to locate their own position outside the classroom.
Science:
Know that different kinds of living things are found in different localities.

investigation

My Aunt Penny says...

Does the size of a woodlice community depend on the stone it lives under? Explain your answer.

4 examining animals

1 examining small animals

The children might like to make a collection of minibeasts, perhaps by shaking them from a tree while holding an umbrella beneath, and using pooters and magnifying boxes to observe them. They could also collect minibeasts from beneath stones, under leaves, on bushes and other plants and even in the house or school. While looking at the creatures closely the children could discover:

★ Do they have legs?
★ How many legs?
★ Do they have wings?
★ How many wings?
★ Do they have a shell?

The children could build up a database of their findings, initially on paper or card, and eventually on a computer or electronic database.

snail's pace

Children have a fascination for snails. They love watching them move and have 'races'. The children could look for, and follow, snail trails in the environment answering the following questions;

★ How far does a snail travel?
★ How can you be sure that you are following the same snail?
★ Do all snails travel the same distance and at the same speed?
★ Do snails move in straight lines?

The children might like to bring some snails into the classroom for a short while and watch them move on different surfaces.

★ Where might the snails leave the 'best' trail? (If the snails are put on black paper they leave quite a distinct trail.)
★ If two snails have a race will the bigger win? How will you decide the winner?

Snails make very co-operative research partners. If a few are collected and marked on their shells with small dots of gloss or emulsion paint, their movements can be tracked and answers found for questions such as:

★ How far do they move in one hour?
★ Which one has moved the farthest?
★ Do they move in a straight line?
★ Do they have a defined territory?

The children can also explore the shape of a snail shell and look for other examples, including sea snails. Children who live near the sea might have the opportunity to follow the trails of winkles at low tide and discover if they move in the same way as land snails. They can also find out if the winkles make similar trails or tracks and whether they move similar distances.

2 examining larger (domestic and farm) animals

Research has found that young children consider that all animals have four legs and fur. Establishing a database about animals they have seen 'for real', in books and on television, might help them develop their concept of 'animal'. The children could look for similarities and differences between, and collect data about, animals, including their own pets, farm animals and perhaps zoo animals. The data could be collated in a variety of ways, from tally, to block graphs and by computer. There are many observations the children can make, much data they could collect, and many ways that the data could be interrogated, so only a few are mentioned here such as:

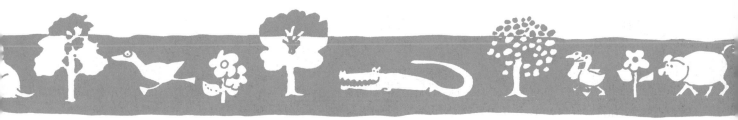

- ★ How many different sorts of 'covering' do these animals have (eg fur, fleece, feathers, scales)?
- ★ Do all animals have four legs?
- ★ How many similarities/differences can you find?
- ★ Do all animals have the same sort of feet?

assessment

Handling Data:
Sort a set of objects describing criteria chosen.
Length:
Comparison. Order.

cross-curricular links

Science:
Sort living things into broad groups according to easily observable features.
Technology:
Design and make a snail 'race track'.
Design, make and use a 'tool' for measuring curves (snail tracks).

investigation

Does the spiral of the snail shell always twist in the same direction?
How do you know?

5   using an animal product

Using Fleece For Spinning, Weaving and Felting
The children are probably aware that sheep are shorn every year. The opportunity to handle a fleece and explore some of the ways in which it can be used and the tactile experiences of feeling its weight, texture and the lanolin on their hands will give a new dimension to their knowledge.

spinning
The children could experiment with spinning the wool into a thread, using a simple home-made spindle. Once they have developed some competence they could:
- ★ Compare the length of their thread with that of other children. They could decide whose is the longest/shortest.
- ★ See if there is a relationship between the length and the thickness of the thread? Is the longest thread the thinnest and the shortest thread the thickest?
- ★ See who can spin the longest thread (which could be a blatantly unfair competition!).
- ★ Develop the idea of a 'fair test' by realising that they need to control the variables, especially the amount of fleece each child starts with.
- ★ Decide on a suitable unit to 'weigh' some fleece for a fair test.
- ★ See who can spin the longest thread in 'fair' conditions.

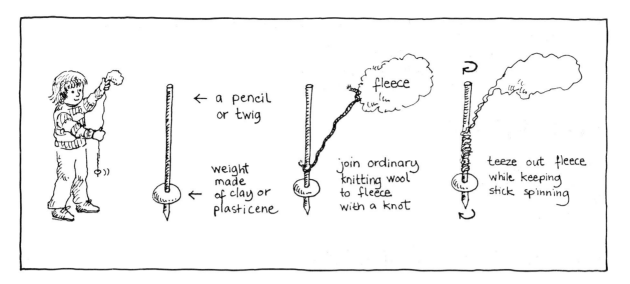

← a pencil or twig

weight made of clay or plasticene

fleece

join ordinary knitting wool to fleece with a knot

teeze out fleece while keeping stick spinning

weaving

The children could examine coarsely woven fabrics, especially tweeds, and look for patterns produced by the weave especially by changing the over/under relationship. They could weave with their own spun thread, or use purchased yarn or thicker threads for ease of handling. The children might like to:

★   Experiment with over/under patterns: Over 1, under 1; over 2, under 1; over 2, under 2 and so on.

★   Look for different over/under combinations in textiles in their own clothing or bought fabrics.

The children could make a rectangle of weaving by setting up the warp threads on hessian stretched in an embroidery ring or simple frame, and using a contrasting coloured thread for the weft. It helps to keep the fabric straight if a stitch is made in the hessian at the end of each 'row'. The finished piece can be measured, backed or mounted and framed. Even young children can make a frame with mitred corners: this could be their introduction to right angles in a meaningful context.

felting

This is a relatively simple one-stage process for turning fibres into cloth which is practised widely in the Central Asian Steppe (especially Afghanistan and Mongolia. Nearer home it is a common material for the making of hats - a good example of its particular characteristics). Because the felting process is less familiar than those of weaving it is described in detail.

felt making

Ideally a fine fleece with a short staple (2.5cm) should be used but other types can be substituted. With young children it may be wise to work outside on swept ground covered with a polythene sheet, or on a table sloping away from the felt-maker to drain off the water.

The fleece should be carded or teased to loosen the fibres, some of which are then placed, with all the fibres lying in one direction, on one half of a piece of calico, canvas or old cotton sheeting leaving a border of about 8cm on the open edges. The second layer is placed with the fibres at right angles to the first and this pattern repeated several times. The calico is then folded in half to make a bag shape and the edges stitched together close to the fleece to hold it in shape (a large piece of felt may need diagonal stitching as well).

The fleece is now ready for the wet stage, known as hardening. Lay the bag on the flat surface (ground, table, plastic tray etc). Wearing rubber gloves sprinkle very hot water over the fleece and using hands or a block of wood press the fleece until all the fibres are

saturated keeping the bag flat meanwhile. (Outside this can be done wearing rubber boots and trampling!). Sprinkle with liquid soap and force this through the fleece. This is particularly important if untreated/unwashed fleece is being used. As the water cools squeeze it out using a rolling pin and sprinkle on some more hot water. This process should be repeated for at least 15 minutes while the felt compresses and hardens.

When the fibres have begun to link together, but before they adhere to the covering, carefully remove the calico. With the fibres matted together the felt is ready for the milling stage.

Milling completes the hardening process. Continue sprinkling with hot water, squeezing with a rolling pin and draining off the cold water until all the fibres are firmly matted. Repeat this process using lots of pressure until you are happy with the appearance of the felt, and finish by drying it.

There are many mathematical activities and concepts encountered during the process:
★   Conservation of weight with reduction in size
★   Measurement of the starting and the finishing thickness of fabric
★   Right angles (The fibres are place at right angles to each other)
★   Area (how much felt can be made from a quantity of fleece and the relationship between area and thickness).

Once a group of children have had the opportunity to make a piece of felt, they become the class 'experts' They can identify the different stages involved in the process, record each stage on a strip of paper and sequence them, thus compiling a flow chart that a subsequent group of felt makers could follow.When the second group of children start the process they should first consult the flow chart. If they have any difficulty in following the instructions or need clarification, they can consult the 'experts'(the first group). Only if they are still having problems should they need to refer to the teacher.

assessment

Handling Data:
Sequencing events in a flow chart.
Shape and Space:
Recognise right angled corners.

cross-curricular links

Art/Craft:
Design and make a small section of wall bonding. Represent in own choice of media.
Geography:
Study locality beyond the U.K. for example the life of nomads living in fabric shelters (tents or yurts). Use of available resources. Ways of life in different environments. Physical geography associated with ponds and the sea shore. Soils and vegetation.
Science:
Compare spinning, weaving and felting. Observe the similarities and differences between woven textiles and felted fabrics. Question whether all animal fibres will felt and spin. Living things: Animals and plants. Technology: Look at whether shelters made from woven or felted materials are similar. Design and making a 'tool' for measuring curved lines (animal tracks)
Art/Craft:
A creative way to use the newly acquired weaving skill would be for children to design and make a small section of wall bonding (See Buildings, Industrialisation and Waste), transfer the design to hessian, and weave each brick using a different colour, or over/under, combination of threads. Observational drawings of plants and animals.

investigation

Are woolly jumpers heavier than synthetic fibre jumpers?
Show me your findings.

6   designing a garden

Many activities involving growing plants are documented elsewhere and will not be repeated here — growing sunflowers for instance. In all these examples there are many opportunities for weighing and measuring, gathering, processing and interrogating data, keeping a time line or diary.

making a garden
There has already been mention of planting trees, shrubs and plants to attract butterflies. The children could design and implement this as a class activity. To make the project their own the children should make as many as possible of the necessary decisions themselves, starting with:
★   Would we like to make a garden?
★   What sort of garden? (butterfly, herb, etc.)
★   Where shall we put our garden?
★   What size should it be?
★   What should it be made of?
★   How can we make it?
★   Which plants and seeds shall we grow?
★   When shall we plant the seeds/plants?
★   How much do plants and seeds cost?
★   How much money would we need?
★   How do we get the money?
★   Should we plant the seeds according to how tall the adult plants will be?

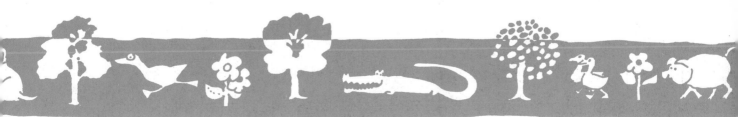

This could become a totally cross-curricular project with a high mathematical content including planning, measuring, organising time, and eventually carrying out the planting. If there are already plant tubs and garden seats scattered around the school environment, the children could see if they are in the most suitable positions by posing questions such as:

★ Could they be in a better place?
★ How could they be arranged?
★ How could we move them from where they are to the new positions?
★ Do we need to get permission before we move them?
★ Can we get permission to move them?

This work could link in with work on Weather or Climate with the children finding the conditions that the plants need. They could also locate the most suitable places in the school grounds with reference to the sunniest spot, the windiest spot etc.

This work could involve making a model, to scale if possible, of the proposed project. The model can be presented and justified to the rest of the school at a 'public' meeting along with maps and plans which, as well as the advertising posters, are made and designed by the children themselves.

home/school links

Ask the children to draw a plan of their own or a friend's garden. In school, using their home plans, they can try to determine the factors which make a garden successful or beautiful by whatever criteria they are using when designing their school garden.

assessment

Length:
Use standard units for measuring.
Money:
Interpret a range of numbers in the context of money.

cross-curricular links

All of this section is effectively a cross-curricular project.

investigation

Do plants grow more by night than by day?
(What did you call night and what did you call day?)
Tell me how you found out about the plants' growth.

7 plants and animals as living things

The focus of this section is on caring for plants and animals rather than on observing and measuring their growth.

home/school link

Children who own pets can keep a record of all the care that their animal needs in, say, one week. In school the children could compare the differing needs of different pets. Some children may be able to do this with farm animals. The children should have the opportunity to find out:

★   When do animals sleep, eat, wash, groom themselves?
★   What does the animal eat? How much does it eat and who feeds it?
★   How much exercise does it need/get each day?
★   Does it exercise itself or does it need to be taken out by people?
★   How much time do people spend each day looking after/ caring for the animals? Who looks after it?
★   How much does it cost to keep the animal for a week?

Children without pets may pursue a similar task with a school pet or by making an arrangement to take a special interest in another child's pet for a short period. Pet owners, even young ones, are often very knowledgeable and happy to share their expertise.

observing trees and plants

To encourage the children to respect the plants in their environment it might be possible for them to 'adopt' a tree, a length of hedgerow or a flower bed in a park or pedestrian shopping centre. They could;

★   Make a complete recording of the locality by mapping and measuring.
★   Make a data collection relating to change over a period of time in number, size etc of plants, animals, condition and litter. This information could be related to seasons or weather.

adopt an animal

It is possible to adopt an animal in a zoo, local park or reserve. The children could keep a record of what the animal eats, how much it eats, when it is active, when its sleeps and its growth. They could compare this data with data about themselves and the data about their pets.

guide dogs

It may be possible for the children to be involved with raising money for a guide dog and to keep in touch with its training, from being a puppy to becoming a blind person's 'eyes'. The children could:

★   Map the puppy's development and training against a time line.
★   Find out how much exercise it needs.
★   Check how far the puppy is walked every day.
★   Compare the puppy's life with their own.

assessment

Handling Data:
Sort a set of objects describing criteria chosen.

cross-curricular links

Geography:
Identify how food needed by the local community is provided.
Where do we obtain the plants that we eat? Local shopping study.
Land use, farming, allotments, gardens. Transport to zoos, farms etc. Seasonal change.

Science:
Explore conditions that living things need to sustain life.

Technology:
Design and make a 'home' for minibeasts or small pets, an adventure playground for a pet, a 'hide' for observing birds or a garden to attract birds outside the classroom window.

investigation

Are cats easier to keep than dogs?
Explain your reasons.

SOILS, ROCKS AND MINERALS

introduction

The activities in this section will help children become more aware of the location of soil and rocks in their environment, the way people use soil and rocks and their importance in people's lives.

Through these mathematical activities, which will encourage the children to handle and examine the materials, they will gain some appreciation of the properties of soil and rocks. This should help to give them some knowledge and understanding for later consideration of the issues listed in Curriculum Guidance 7 (Resource limitation; management of resources; soil erosion, fertility and conservation; and the effects of the extractive industry).

discussion points

What is soil?
Where would you find soil?
Can you make soil?
Is all soil brown?
Who uses soil?
What do they use soil for?
Why is sand good to play with?

What are rocks?
Are rocks the same as stones and pebbles?
Where can you find rocks?
How are rocks made?
What do we use rocks for?
What colour are the rocks?
Are all rocks the same?

soils and rocks

1   **Exploring** soil and rocks
2   **Visiting** a farm or market garden
3   **Visiting** a park, garden or wood
4   **Visiting** the coast
5   **Visiting** a quarry
6   **Examining** soils and rocks
7   **Growing** things in soil

resources and preparation

Prepare a collection of soils and soil-like materials, weights, non-standard weights etc. assorted pots and containers, a range of meshes from chicken wire (or something coarser) to carpet canvas and net; plus fine elastic bands, tape, adhesives etc. Children should wear gloves when handling soil.

1 exploring soils and rocks

Children should have opportunities to explore and experience the properties of rocks and soils through play. Allowing for health considerations there is a wide range of materials that could be used, for example:

Soils, beach sand (including pebbles), gravel (both angular and rounded), peat, assorted potting composts (both soil and peat based), locally-derived materials like China clay waste (contains quartz crystals), coarse red sands and sandy soils and many more, with different colours, textures, compositions and even smells!

inside

Activities may be centred around sand trays, small bowls, troughs etc as available, filled with the above. The children can be invited to consider these situations and questions:

★   Create landscapes, islands, gardens, hills. Will all the materials make good shapes — like hills?
★   Can you pour all the materials. Do they all flow well? Do they flow from different heights?
★   Build sand castles. Are some materials better than others to use? Which are best?
★   Make shakers. Do they all make the same noise? Can you describe the noise?
★   Move the material around with hands, spoons and sticks. Will it squash? Does it feel heavy?
★   Do you prefer wet or dry material? What does it feel like?
★   When you pour water on where does it go? What happens to the material?

outside

Around the school the children can have the opportunity to dig in a garden, flower bed, tub or grow bag. Large tyres can be filled with soil. The children should have the opportunity to dig in the garden at different times of the year, in different weather conditions and with different tools. The children may be invited to consider these situations and questions:

★   Make a deep hole. How deep is it?
★   Do some weeding. How many different types of weeds have you found?
★   Pick out the stones. Are they all the same size?
★   Riddle (sieve) the soil. Do you always sieve out stones?
★   Mix some sand with the soil. Where does the sand go?

assessment

No extras.

cross-curricular links

English:
Participate as speakers and listeners in a group engaged in a given task.

investigation

Is it easy to dig a hole in any soil?
Tell me what you found.

2 visiting a farm or market garden

Children should have the opportunity to see soil and rocks in the natural environment. Video material might be appropriate for rocks and soils in distant places. On all the visits the children should be shown how to collect a reasonable sample for use later back at school. They could mark on a simple map the location of each specimen.

Ask the children to:
★ Look at the farmer's/market gardener's fields. Are they all the same colour?
★ Look at the soil. Are there stones in it? Are there many stones? What shape and colour are they? Where are the stones? Are they evenly distributed? Can the children see anything else in the soil?
★ Ask the farmer how he 'digs' his field. Can he explain about ploughing, harrowing and drilling?
★ Observe the furrows, the lines they make across the field and their shape in cross section. Why are they this shape? They could decide which arbitrary unit to use to measure the separation of the furrows and their height (depth). Do parallel furrows ever meet?
★ Estimate how far apart the seeds/plants will be placed by looking at the farmer's machinery used for this purpose?
★ Look at the plants already growing in the fields. Are the furrows still visible? Are the plants growing in the peaks or the troughs?
★ Ask the farmer when he ploughs his fields, when he plants his seeds, when he harvests his crop and whether the crop is put in sacks or boxes etc
★ Look at the pasture land. Is there any soil in this? Where is it?

The children can collect some soil and on returning to school they can use the soil for the processes in **EXAMINING SOIL**. They can also make a chart to depict the farmer's year. Younger children can make a zig zag book which depicts the farmer's year.

assessment

Shape and Space:
Use language related to parallel lines.
Time:
Order events using a calendar.

cross-curricular links

Geography:
Find the farm to be visited on a large scale map.

History:
Look at old farming instruments, especially those used to prepare soil.
Technology:
Design a tool for measuring depth (of furrows).

investigation

If you plant the same sort of seed in each of the soils you have collected will they all grow equally well?
Show me how you know.

3   visiting a park/garden or a wood

park or garden
Before making the visit ask the children to identify the things they think that they will find at a park or in a garden.

At the park or garden ask the children:
★   To identify any soil or rocks and sketch the shape of any flower beds or borders.
★   To note what is growing in the flower beds or borders. Are the flowers planted in any pattern?
★   To look carefully at the grass to see if it is growing and what it is growing in/on. What happens when too many people walk on the grass? How do you know?
★   About stones or rocks anywhere else but in the soil. Are there any buildings made of stone or rock. What shapes are the rocks or stones? Are they the same shape as the rocks and stones in the soil? How do they fit together?

The children can collect some soil and on return to school they can examine it as in **EXAMINING SOIL**. They can also record their findings by mapping and tallying or they can choose their own method of recording.

wood
(Allow for the usual health considerations.)
The children can explore the ground beneath the trees — using plastic gloves if necessary. The children can be invited to consider these situations and questions:
★   What does it feel like?
★   Does it have a smell?
★   Is the ground wet or dry?
★   Is it stony or rocky? Are the stones big or small?
★   What is it made of? Are there any leaves in it? Do the leaves in the ground match the leaves in the trees round about?
★   How far in the ground can you push your fingers? Is the ground hard or soft?
★   Look at the leaves on the ground. Lift them gently. Are they all the same shape? Are all the leaves whole?
★   What is underneath one of the leaves on the ground?
★   Is there anything living in the soil?
★   Is there anything else in the soil? Are there twigs, nuts and/or fruit?
They can also collect a soil sample to take back to school. On return to school the children can use decision trees or Venn/Carroll diagrams to record their findings.

assessment

Handling Data:
Sort a set of objects describing criteria chosen.

cross-curricular links

Geography:
Identify familiar landscape features, including ponds and woods, and explore different gradients of slope.
Describe an activity designed to improve a place the children have visited.

investigation

My brother David says...

Is a quarter of all soil stones? Show me your evidence.

4   visiting the coast

If you have the choice try to select a beach that has a wide variety of materials - not just the best sand around. Give the children the opportunity to explore the variety of beach materials, to describe it, play with it, dig, pour, use it wet and dry.

When the children have played, ask them to:
★   Collect as many stones as they can. Encourage them to look for different colours and patterns. They can also choose their favourite stone and the one that feels the roughest and/or the smoothest.
★   Look at the shapes of the pebbles on the beach. Are they rounded or angular? What makes the pebbles on a beach round and smooth?
★   Try to pick dry sand in handfuls. Can you pick up wet sand?
★   See what happens when you drop wet sand from a height?
★   Look at the colour of the sand. Is it always the same colour?
★   See who can make a circular pattern in the sand.

* ★ Make a pattern in the sand using straight lines.
* ★ Try to make a maze. Can everyone get to the centre of the maze?

The children can collect a large pebble and back in school they can be asked to:
* ★ Find out who has the largest pebble.
* ★ Choose five pebbles and arrange them in order. Now take a sixth pebble and place that in the correct order of sequence.

(Pebbles should not be removed from beaches in large quantities. After they have been used in the classroom, an effort should be made to return them to the place they were taken from.)

assessment

Shape and Space:
Use language related to movement and position.
Volume:
Order by estimation.

cross-curricular links

Art:
Draw, make patterns, collages based on shells and shell shapes and artwork using shells.
Geography:
Express personal likes and dislikes about features of the locality.
Describe ways in which people have changed the environment.

investigation

Can you investigate sorting 16 pebbles up a decision tree?
Show me your trees.

5   visiting a quarry

(NB Quarries can be dangerous places!)
Let the children explore and then ask them to consider these situations and questions:
* ★ Why is the quarry like a hole in the ground?
* ★ What has been taken away to make the hole? Why has the material been moved?
* ★ Can you see any patterns in the rock? They may see sets of parallel layers (bedding planes); they may see curved patterns (possibly folds); they may notice changes of rock type indicated by change of colour, texture, feel; they may notice fossils.
* ★ Consider the size and shape of the quarry. Can the quarry get any bigger? How? Why?
* ★ Can the rim of the quarry get any bigger?
* ★ Are all the walls of the quarry as steep as each other?
* ★ How do people get down into the quarry and out again?
* ★ If there are any machines, vehicles or buildings the children can make drawings of them.

- ★ Are there any lorries. What do you notice about their size/construction?
- ★ Compare the rock on the walls of the quarry with the rock that has been broken up.
- ★ Can you find out what the rock is being quarried for and who is going to use it?
- ★ Find the biggest rock. Measure it for height, width, girth and weight. The measurements can still be estimated even if it is impossible to do any practical measurements.

assessment

Length:
Use arbitrary or standard units.

cross-curricular links

Art:
Make a collection of aesthetically pleasing rocks.
Geography:
Identify and name materials obtained from natural resources.
Identify how people obtain materials from the environment.
Describe effects on the environment of extracting natural resources.
Technology:
Design a vehicle for carrying heavy loads.

investigation

Is rock always heavy to move and carry?
Tell me how you made your decision.

6   examining soils

sieving

Ask the children what they think soil is made of, and also if all soils are the same. For this activity use the material collected on visits, or specially collected from different places such as gardens, woodland, moorland, growbag, farm field or whatever your locality can provide (taking the usual health precautions). Remember to return the soil after the experiments.

Using material from your collection ask the children to:
- ★ Sort out by hand the different materials they can see – they might pick out twigs, stones, leaves, roots etc.
- ★ Sort the soil mechanically by sieving. The children can use domestic sieves like colanders, tea strainers, flour sieves, garden riddles etc with a wide variety of mesh sizes. The children should use two or more sieves for successive sievings. The sievings can then be compared.
- ★ Compare their sievings with the sievings of other children. The children should comment on the presence or absence of leaves, stones etc., the proportion of different grades of material, the colour of the different soils and the grades of the material.

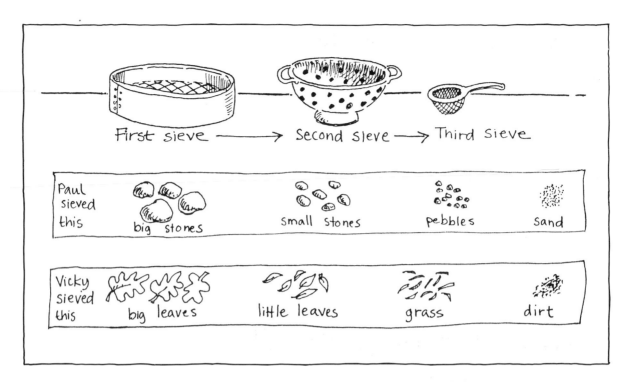

The children should talk about their work. This discussion should lead to the children using the language of AREA when they are talking about the holes they dig, the VOLUME of the amount of the different particles and the PROPORTION of each sieving.

weighing

Ask the children to weigh out a kilo (or a large arbitrary unit) of soil. Using this sample ask the children to:

★ Sieve the soil, using two or more sieves, as above, then weigh each sieving fraction using any chosen unit.

★ Repeat with other soils, starting with the same quantity. The children could record their findings as a block graph, one column for each sieving fraction, and one block graph for each soil.

★ Compare and describe the bar charts for each different soil by asking questions such as: How heavy was the sample to start with? How heavy was each sieving fraction? How heavy were all the sieving fractions for one sample altogether? Did half/quarter of the soil fall through the first sieve each time? Did the largest particles weigh the most?

This activity could be repeated using coarser material made up of obvious rock fragments, such as gravel, beach pebbles, aggregate, China clay waste or any similar locally derived material.

assessment

Volume:
Comparison of proportions.
Weight:
Use standard units for measuring.

cross-curricular links

Technology:
Design, make and test a sieving system.
Design make and use another system for sorting soil into its constituents.
Science:
Investigate the sievings for evidence of minibeasts.

investigation

Are all soils the same?
How do you know.

7   growing things in soil

gardening - growing things

The children should experience the excitement of growing their own plants in pots or in the school garden beds, tubs or growbags before commencing any structured work where they need to be more patient or controlled.

Ask the children to:
★   Plant a large seed (bean, pea, nasturtium), look after it and keep a record in the form of a diary or a height chart like those sold to record a child's growth. The children could decide how to record the growth or (if appropriate) they could record in terms of counting the number of leaves or flowers.

Growing 'Fair Test'

Ask the children if plants grow just as well in all soils and if they grow at the same rate. Then set up a 'fair test' perhaps by setting up something blatantly unfair at first. Discuss with the children how to make it fair. They can use their measuring, recording and computational skills to:
★   Fill several yoghurt pots each with a different soil, and plant the same type of seed and the same number in each at the same depth etc.
★   Devise a way of treating each plant the same fair way and measure and record the visible growth of each plant. Later the children can discuss the likelihood of the biggest plants having the largest roots. They can keep a diary of their experiments and be encouraged to reach conclusions.

home/school links

growing outside

Ask the children to find some acorns or sycamore keys when out for a walk with their parents. In school the children can discuss where they think that the acorns and sycamore seeds will grow best. The fruits can then be planted in dry, wet, sunny places etc.and the locations recorded on a map or plan. A growth diary or a report can be discussed and compared on the same day each week. The children could also grow acorns in the classroom and transplant them outside later.

assessment

Length: Use standard units for measuring.

cross-curricular links

English:
Present a TV gardening programme as a role play activity reporting on the different growing media in terms of growth rate.
Science:
Know that certain things need certain conditions to sustain life.
Technology:
Design a fair way to water the plants.

investigation

WATER

introduction

This section is intended to raise children's awareness of water; where it comes from and the importance of water to our lives and those of plants and animals. The children are encouraged to become aware of the properties of water through play activities. The activities in this section can be timed to coincide with the routine experiences of using and understanding liquid measures. Visits will increase their knowledge of where water may be found, and on their visits they will observe and record through mathematical activities the flora and fauna which depend upon water. These observations and recordings could be part of a longer term study. Before these visits children will need to be made aware of the flora and fauna of which they could find evidence.

discussion points

Where can you find water?
Where can you find lots of water?
Where can you find a little water?
What does it feel like?
How does water look?
Does water make patterns?
What do the patterns look like?

water

1   **Exploring** water
2   **Observing** water
3   **Catching** water
4   **Planning** a visit to water
5   **Visiting** water
6   **Using** water

resources and preparations

Water trays and a selection of tea strainers, teapots, watering cans, yogurt pots, hand cream dispensers, straws, pebbles, tights or stockings, feathers, fabrics etc. A collection of pictures from magazines etc depicting a variety of scenes but including some which show water.

A collection of suitable containers for catching water. For example: plastic trays, litre lemonade bottles with the tops cut off and turned upside in the lower portion to serve as funnels; bowls of various sizes; two large, clean, dustbins or barrels - ideally one of which could be placed to catch the water coming down a drainpipe. (Children may see the advantages of using this water for their garden and pot plants rather than using water from a tap.) A collection of bottles of differing capacities, each with a manufacturer's label indicating its capacity in 'mls'.

1   exploring water

Children should have opportunities to explore and experience the properties of water through play. The expression of sensations and ideas, and conversations between children and with adults during the play sessions will lead to the mathematics. Activities may be centred on water trays, small bowls, troughs etc as available. The children may be invited to look at things that can happen to water and describe or record their ideas. Consider these situations and questions:

★ Make waves — What shape are they? — Do they make a sound?
★ Make the water move with fingers, hands — What shapes do you make?
★ Move the water with spoons, tea strainers, a piece of cloth — Can you see what happens?
★ Pump water using hand cream dispensers — Can you see what happens?
★ Pour water from different heights using different sized roses on watering cans, different sized teapots — What happens? What can you hear? Do you always get the same amount of water?
★ Blow on the surface of the water through cardboard tubes, straws etc — What happens?
★ Drop pebbles, feathers, sticks etc into the water — What happens?
★ Soak pieces of different materials in water, then squeeze them — How much water comes from each piece? (Try wool, cotton- wool, chamois leather, fur, velvet, silk, flannel, plastic, sponges, foam rubber etc.)

assessment

Capacity:
Compare and order objects without measuring.

cross-curricular links

Art:
Design ripple patterns.
English:
Draw a picture about your activity and write about it.
Science:
Use syphons and pipettes to move things.

investigation

Are wet things always heavier than dry things?
Explain what you have found out to me.

2   observing water

where does water come from?

On a rainy day observe the precipitation. Discuss: "Where is the rain coming from?" — "What is the likelihood of it raining all day today/tomorrow?" (The same could be done on a snowy day.) During the course of a week keep a chart which records the children's conjectures on the next day's weather and compare with what happens.

where does the water go?

On a rainy day watch the water. Where does the water go? Why are there puddles? When it stops raining ask the children to draw around a puddle with a piece of chalk and measure the size of the puddle using arbitrary units of measure or centimetres. They can return to the puddle at timed intervals throughout the day to take further measurements. Discuss where the water has gone.

measure and chalk a line around perimeter of a puddle

return to measure again at intervals

Where does water go in the countryside?

The children can sort a collection of pictures showing country scenes. Some may show puddles, streams, rivers or springs while others depict various aspects of country life. Ask the children to give the reasons for their sorting.

assessment

Probability:
Recognise outcomes can vary.
Handling Data:
Sort a set of pictures.

Length (width, diameter, perimeter etc):
Measure using appropriate units.
Area:
Measure using appropriate units.

cross-curricular links

Geography:
Observe and identify the forms in which water naturally occurs in the environment.
Observe and describe what happens to water when it reaches the ground.
Technology:
Design and make a device for measuring the depth of water in a puddle.

investigation

Can puddles form anywhere?
Explain what you have found out to me.

3   catching water

outside

On a rainy day the children can choose a container from the selection described in RESOURCES which they place somewhere outside to catch water. After a suitable length of time, the containers should be brought together and the children given an opportunity to measure the contents with their own choice of units. This may usefully be followed by a comparison of the amounts collected by others with the children being allowed to choose direct comparison, arbitrary units or bottles from the collection using these as measures. Locations and quantities should stimulate important mathematical ideas such as conservation and volume. It should be noted that the standard which the children use, whether volume or depth of water, cannot be related to the figures used in Weather Forecasts.

Following these discussions it may be useful to investigate the amount of rainfall over a longer time span, collecting, measuring and recording rainfall. The children can decide if they want to measure using volume or to compare depths.

inside

With the co-operation of the School Caretaker the children should be able to discover if and where the mains water supply to the school is metered. If it can be located, they may be able to obtain or derive some data about total quantities used and levels of consumption throughout the day. They may be asked to consider why the supply is metered and what the implications of this might be for the school and for them as individuals, with thoughts about waste from careless use, dripping taps etc. If there is a dripping tap they may like to quantify the water wasted in this way.

assessment

Capacity:
Compare, order and measure using appropriate units.

cross-curricular links

Education for economic and industrial understanding:
Discuss the people and industrial processes involved in providing water for our taps.

investigation

My cousin Runvir says...

When I wash my hands I sometimes put the plug in and sometimes I don't.
Which way uses less water?
Explain your answer to me.

4   planning a visit to water

You might like to consider, in the light of local knowledge and opportunities, one or more of the following:

River	Canal	Stream	Spring	
Reservoir	Waterworks	Seaside	Harbour	Docks

Try to make at least two visits if possible: one where the movement of the water is natural, and one where it has been contained or constrained by human endeavour. As well as the spontaneous conversations that will take place during the visits, the children may be guided towards certain specific observations or asked to fulfil tasks which will provide the basis for subsequent mathematical activities.

planning

The maximum involvement of the children in the planning stages of any visit is important and should itself represent a significant and rewarding experience. This involvement might include an examination of the school calendar to choose suitable dates, writing letters where permission is required, letters to parents, assessing the seating capacity of transport required, sources of transport, costs involved, timing of journeys etc in relation to distances and possible needs to suit tide times, arrangements for the collection of any contributions to be requested, pocket money, meals, lists of things to take, advice about what to wear and so

on... Ideally the children should arrive at a point where they feel they are organising their own visit not being 'taken' on a trip. The representation and display of this work as an illustrated class calendar might also be undertaken.

projecting

Younger children might like to make a frieze or zig-zag book showing what they expect to do and see on the visit, and discuss those things which they think are certain to happen and those which are uncertain. Their conjectures could be compared with a similar presentation made after the event.

assessment

Money:
Solve problems involving money.
Solve problems involving coach capacity.
Length:
Estimate, measure and calculate (from scale on map).
Handling Data:
Access information in a simple time/tide table.
Probability:
Recognise that there is a degree of uncertainty about the outcome of some events but that others are certain or impossible.

cross-curricular links

English:
Make lists of the items needed to take from school and home for the visit — including the packed lunch.
Letter writing.
Geography:
Find on a map the place to be visited.
Identify land, sea and other areas of water on maps and globes.

investigation

Your trip will cost ... In how many ways can you pay for it?
Show me all your answers.

5   visiting water

recording

The children will need a small booklet in which to write or some A5 sheets of paper. The younger children may be asked to draw:
★   Something too big to put your arms around
★   Something taller than yourself
★   Something smaller than yourself
★   Something taken by people to that place and left.

The older children may be asked to draw:
- ★ The shape of a fish if they can see one
- ★ A flower
- ★ A tree
- ★ The footprint of an animal coming to that place for water
- ★ Something taken by people to that place and left.

Back in the classroom the children can use the sorting diagrams to identify and classify their drawings. The discussion needs to establish that there are differences in plants and animals: some plants are only found in and around water; some creatures need water to live in, and others only need to visit water.

measuring
While at the water the children can mark out a metre square and record the number of rocks, plants, feathers, bones, flowers etc found in it. This information could become part of an on-going project visiting the same spot periodically. Where possible this information might be recorded on a database so that it can be interrogated over a longer period of time.

playing
Where there is a bridge or safe access to running water play 'Pooh Sticks'. This activity should promote discussion about how the race is measured and won, and provide a good introduction to ideas about speed and the use of "instruments" for measuring distance and time.

examining
The children can be asked to look at the surface of the water and asked questions such as:
- ★ Does the surface always react in the same way as the surface of the water in the school sand tray when it is blown or when pebbles are dropped in it?
- ★ What can you see reflected in the water?
- ★ What does the reflection look like on a wavy surface/a smooth surface?
- ★ What shape are the edges of the water?

assessment

Length:
Estimate and measure.
Time:
Use a clock.
Handling Data:
Design a data collection sheet, record and interrogate data.
Shape and Space:
Recognise symmetry as reflection.

cross-curricular links

Art:
Recreate on paper the images seen in the water. Cut the picture into wavy lines, place on a larger sheet of paper with spaces to create the effect of ripples.
Geography:
Identify and use geographical language to talk about landscape features.
Science:
Living things need certain conditions for life including water.

investigation

Grandma Peg says...

Can water go up a hill? Explain your answer to me.

6   using water

home/school link

The children may be asked to measure how much water they use in the bath using a litre fruit squash bottle or plastic measuring jug as a standard unit. This exercise could be a good starting point for the examination of individual daily water consumption. This might also be a good time to discuss the possibilities for the re-use of bath water in times of shortage.

drinking

The children can be asked to consider ways of identifying and recording the amount of water they drink or otherwise consume each day, both as individuals and in more collective ways (water for cooking food, water for cleaning the school/home etc).

problem solving

Can the children solve this problem?
The Dinner Ladies are taking far too much water into the dining hall at dinner time and are throwing it away at the end of the meal. Can the children find out how much water is needed and avoid waste? This might well be used as a group activity and so produce several solutions or suggestions, the merits or otherwise of each being discussed by the whole class with, perhaps, one or more of the Dinner Ladies taking part. Remember it is the mathematical journey that counts — getting an answer is a bonus!

assessment

Capacity:
Recognise the need for standard units.
Number:
Calculate using any or all of the operations.
Handling Data:
Collect, record and interpret data.

cross-curricular links

English:
List all the uses for water.
History:
Investigate how water was used as a source of power.
Science:
Investigate the factors affecting floating and sinking and how they enable goods to be transported by water.
Technology:
Find where the piped water supply enters the home and where waste water leaves the home.

investigation

How much water do you drink at lunchtime during the school year?
Explain your answer to me.

INFORMATION

some of the mathematical background

Whilst this is not a mathematics text book in a formal sense, it has been decided to provide information and reference on some of the general working methods and processes mentioned in the activities, and more especially with regard to the developmental sequence of techniques for the collection and representation of data.

writing down mathematics

When writing down the results of mathematical thinking there are two aspects to be considered — the personal and the public.

The personal serves as an aide-mémoir. During the solving of a problem, people often jot things down so that what is already thought or concluded is not forgotten. This jotting can be on scraps of paper or the backs of envelopes: any rough scrap will do, because the digits or notes are personal and their relevance to the task in hand understood, although they may be rough or untidy. It is essential that children acquire these 'back of envelope' skills and the habit of keeping track of their thinking and progress during mathematical processes.

Nevertheless, when producing work for public use we are forced to consider the symbols, conventions and formats for displaying our data. This need to communicate with precision and intelligibility means that children must learn and use the accepted systems for recording their mathematics.

Children will need to produce evidence for teachers and assessors to show that they have understood the mathematical processes and can correctly reach conclusions. They also need to produce work that helps the teacher to diagnose problems. These needs can be met by both personal and public methods of recording, with the former requiring the children's explanations and interpretations. These explanations will not only allow the teacher to diagnose any problems more clearly and effectively, but may also enable the children to correct their own misunderstandings or errors.

The Non-statutory Guidance of the National Curriculum suggests that teachers offer children group problem solving activities, paired investigations, individual work, practical, oral and written tasks, and through these teaching strategies encourage children to create their own formats for displaying their results or presenting their work in a visual way. Time should also be found by the teacher to discuss the children's results and the children encouraged to explain their own and other children's work.

The Non-statutory Guidance also says that children should develop mental agility and be able to perform calculations mentally. This approach is wholeheartedly endorsed in this book and therefore prescribed formats are not shown in the activities. These are for teachers and the children to negotiate and agree.

As already discussed children will need to become familiar with conventional formats and layouts and also have opportunities to see mathematics in action. Much emphasis is placed on children seeing adults, including teachers, read purposefully and for pleasure. In the same way teachers need to be seen using mathematics publicly in a routine way — counting money for a charity collection or for a trip, or calculating dinner numbers. Parents also need to be reminded to use mathematics more in front of the children, even if it is just on the simple level of writing out a shopping list to see how much money will be needed, or sharing with them the cash transactions of purchases.

On other occasions children should see that mathematics can be used for fascination and for fun and that grownups can employ an investigation, for instance when they work out how many miles the new car is doing to the litre or how much it costs to get to work.
Other investigations the teacher might share are:
★ How many meals have you cooked in your lifetime?
★ How many years have you spent in bed?
★ Look at your house number. What questions could you ask about it? If it has more than two digits what happens if you reverse the digits and then subtract the smaller number from the larger? Repeat that process of reversal and subtraction several times. What happens? Would it be the same for all the children in the class? (They may need to use a calculator but they will enjoy joining in the investigation.)

handling data
When studying the environment, or using it as a starting point for mathematical activity, much of the mathematics comes into the category of 'Handling Data'.
The children will need to:
★ Collect information
★ Represent or record their findings
★ Interpret their records in order to draw conclusions or discover relationships
★ Communicate their findings and ideas to other children, parents or a wider public.

collecting information
When seeking information the children will need to be clear about what data they need to collect during any given task and how they are to collect it. When collecting data children may use one of the following skills depending on the situation and the child's ability:
★ Counting objects by one-to-one correspondence, representing each object with a bead or stone put into a yoghurt pot or some other container.
★ Sorting
★ Tallying (the 5 bar gate idea ⊞), counting objects without forgetting where you are in the count. There are push-button gadgets which can be purchased for this purpose which are particularly useful in something like a traffic survey where speed is important. However the manual skill of tallying is very important and should be included in children's mathematical experiences.

representing and recording data
Children should be encouraged to create their own systems of representation without the teacher giving ideas or indications at the start. It is through experimenting that they will become aware of and see the need for standard forms of representation. Data can be displayed as lists, organised tables, grid/matrices, diagrams or graphs. All representations require titles to help others understand the topic under investigation. Many will require other labels to identify further subdivisions or details.

sorting

Sorting requires observation and language. Children need to be able to talk about similarities and differences. They also need to be able to isolate one attribute at a time and apply it systematically to each item of the set being studied. The results of sorting are usually shown on Carroll Diagrams, (these diagrams are named after Lewis Carroll who wrote Alice in Wonderland), on Venn diagrams or on decision trees. All these diagrams require children to ask a Yes/No question or to look for an attribute which each item in the set either has or lacks.

When young children first meet these diagrams it makes sense to introduce them by getting them to sort themselves or something they know well, such as their toys.
The children can sort themselves by asking:
★　　　Are you a boy?
★　　　Are you wearing trainers?
★　　　Does your coat have a hood?

This information can be displayed as follows:

Caroll & Venn diagrams
A **one decision** Caroll or Venn diagram has one line and sorts the collection into two subsets.

Carroll

Venn

boy	~~boy~~
Adam Steve Peter Joe	Mary Juanita Sue

Juanita　　　　　Mary
boy
(Adam
Steve
Peter
Sue　　Joe)

A **two decision** Carroll diagram or Venn diagram has two lines and sorts the collection into four subsets.

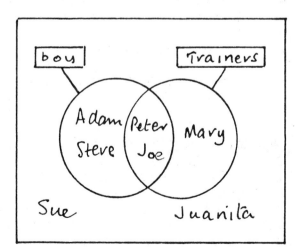

	boy	~~boy~~
~~Trainers~~	Adam Steve	Juanita Sue
Trainers	Peter Joe	Mary

A **three decision** diagram has three lines and sorts the collection into eight subsets.

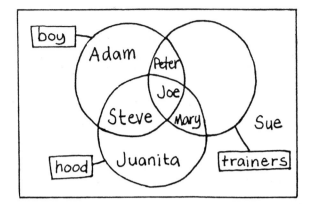

Note 1. Carroll decided that 'not boy' was denoted by b̶o̶y̶ although the National Curriculum allows 'not boy' as a label Note 2. Venn circles contain those items which HAVE the attribute shown by the label. The objects which DO NOT possess the attribute are in the region outside the circle. The surrounding "background" is the important region for those items which display NONE of the attributes under scrutiny.

Tree Diagrams

A tree diagram, which sorts a structured logic set such as Logiblocs or People, looks like a family tree but has the same question repeated on every branch of any one 'generation', and through every generation. To prepare children for assessment at level 4 (NAT5 4e) in the use of tree diagrams it is necessary that they should be using simplified trees at an early age.

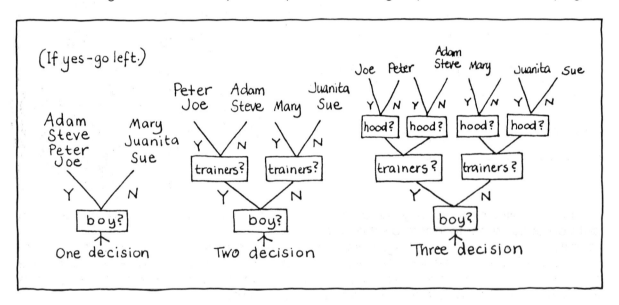

This is different from an identification or classification tree (often used in Science) when both sides do not necessarily need to contain the same question as there may be no objects in the collection to warrant the inclusion. At first the children usually leave the objects sorted on display as a record of their sort. At a later stage they can leave drawings or representations of the sorted objects on their diagrams. It is usual practice to encourage the children to transfer their items for sorting from one diagram to another so that they can make the connections between the different types of diagrams.

computer sorting

The computer program 'Branch' is useful in the classroom after the children have had a great deal of practical work sorting 'real life items' and logic material up the decision trees.

The National Curriculum in NAT5 Programme of Study expects children to be able to:
- ★   Select criteria for sorting a set of objects and apply them consistently.
- ★   Record with real objects or drawings and comment about the result.
- ★   Choose criteria to sort and classify objects, record results or outcomes of events.
- ★   Use diagrams to represent the result of classification using two different criteria.
- ★   Create a decision tree diagram with questions to sort and identify collections of objects.

The children should always be encouraged to talk about their representations and ask questions about the facts represented in the diagrams.

the matrix grid

The matrix grid is a useful diagram easily mastered by children for identifying the elements of a set. Using commercial sets such as Logiblocs, Logic People, House sorts, What's in a square? etc, is a very easy way into this form of recording. Children can then be encouraged to make their own sets by starting with a blank grid and creating their own headings.

Logiblocs (small pieces only)

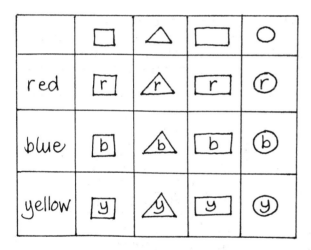

What's in a Square?

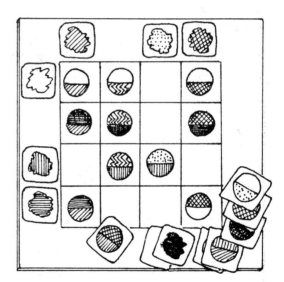

This links well with the use of organised tables and lists as in the National Curriculum, "Design a data collection sheet to record a set of data leading to a frequency table" and also "Extract specific pieces of information from tables and lists". At this point children say that this last item is a "yellow circle" ie. reading the vertical axis before the horizontal. Later, of course, we apply the convention of the horizontal being the first coordinate. However, when using tables the convention of reading the vertical axis first often applies.

counting

Counting objects requires a different form of representation. The number of objects in each subset in the sorting diagrams above would prove tedious to count if the numbers in the collection were large. Frequency tables need to be created which show the reader 'how many' easily and efficiently. We therefore have pictograms, block graphs, barcharts and later, histograms, pie charts, and bar-line graphs.

pictograms

The lines of pictograms can be vertical or horizontal. The lines do not need to touch. If the children cut out their own and glue them there is a danger of distortion in that 3 elephants might look longer than 6 mice.

Our favourite animal

(i)   (ii)

Mathematically the chart (i) displays the correct information but the visual perception can be misleading. The children should be helped to see the drawback for themselves and realise that the pictures should be drawn on the same sized pieces of paper as in diagram (ii) or the pictures should be stuck into standard spaces of the chart.

block graphs

These differ from barcharts in the way they are constructed. The final product may look like a bar chart but it is created block by block. The principle of one-to-one correspondence is used. Each child colours in one square or first places a cube to represent himself on the chart. A count of how many children, say, prefer the colour blue, is not made until the end of the chart construction.

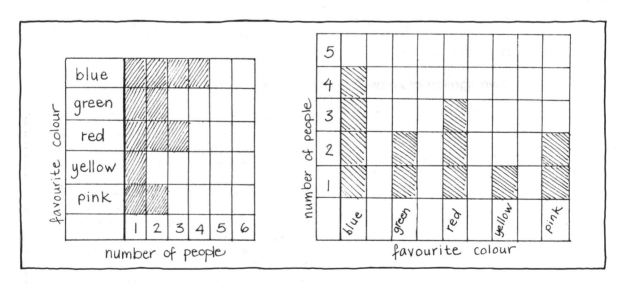

Class 4's favourite colour

Because it is constructed block by block the count labels are associated with the blocks and not the lines. The numbers, when they are eventually included, go in the spaces and not on the lines. The 'bars' can go vertically or horizontally and they do not necessarily have to be touching. In order that there is no perceived mis-information, it is customary that the bars are all the same width. The National Curriculum expects children to "construct and interpret frequency tables and block graphs."

bar charts

Again the bars can be horizontal or vertical and they do not need to touch. They do not need to be the same width but it is customary and less misleading to make them so. In constructing a bar chart it is usual to count all the members in the subset and enter the bar in one count/action. We are, therefore, immediately aware of the total needed in the whole bar. The need to be able to read the height/length of the bar quickly becomes obvious. For this reason the frequency axis is labelled on the lines not the squares.

Number of cars of different colours passing a given spot in 10 minutes.

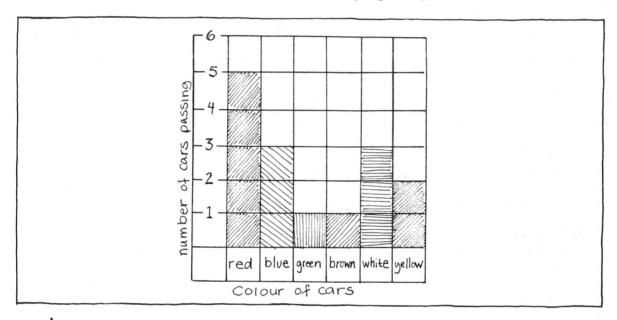

scale

When the count becomes too great for a pictogram or for one-to-one correspondence of the squares on the graph paper, then a scale must be introduced. Sometimes this can be seen in the use of symbols in a table.

Investigation into types of footwear worn by Class 1 to school

sandals	
lace ups	
trainers	
daps	
slippers	

Scale: represents 5 children
(each head and each limb=1 child)

The National Curriculum expects that children can construct and interpret bar charts, graphs and pictograms where one square represents a group of units. Scale can of course be introduced to bar charts in the usual way where one square, initially, represents a count of two items. More advanced forms of count/frequency graphs are dealt with after Key Stage 1.

relationship diagrams
Relationship diagrams have only a small space in Key Stage 1. Children at this age find it difficult to look at two variables at once and discover trends. However, we can lay the foundations for work such as scattergraphs, line graphs and harder barcharts leading to an understanding of average and normal distribution.

mapping diagrams
The simple mapping diagram is much used with young children.

Eg. What energy does the gadget need to make it work?

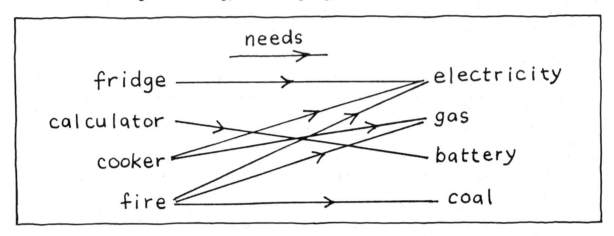

The National Curriculum expects that children can create simple mapping diagrams showing relationships and interpret them.

interrogating and interpreting the results
Creating a pictorial representation is only part of the process of handling data. In adult life there is a frequent need to interpret data collected and presented by others in the communications media. Interpreting and questioning the pictograms or barcharts is an important skill for life. Children must learn to ask questions about the graph from the very beginning. "Tell me something about this graph" is an essential injunction in every teacher's repertoire.

For example, imagine that class 4 are looking at the chart which shows their favourite colour (see page 96). The children must be encouraged to be able to express the sort of ideas which are inherent in the following statements. They are listed in an approximate order of mathematical complexity.

"Blue is the favourite colour in Class 4."
"More children prefer blue than red."
"Yellow is the least popular colour in class 4."
"One more person prefers blue to red."
"The same number of people like green and pink."
"One fewer person likes red rather than blue."
"Twelve children took part in this survey."
"Six children were away today. If you add their results blue may not be the favourite colour any more."

"This chart means that we might have to buy more blue and red crayons than yellow."
"The results in Class 5 may be very different."

Referring to the mapping diagram for **ENERGY** (see page 98), questions asked here could lead to statements such as:
"Fires are things which can be worked by most sorts of energy."
"Homes will probably have to have more than one type of energy source eg. electricity and batteries."

The teacher should take every opportunity to introduce charts published in papers, comics etc. With very young children, just knowing that they exist will be enough, but older children can start to interpret this published data and begin to draw sensible and critical conclusions. The National Curriculum places a great emphasis on the skill of interpretation and expects children to be able to record and comment about the results; to read and interpret them (Mapping diagrams); to read and interpret block graphs and frequency tables; to interpret bar charts; to interpret graphs (pictograms) where the symbol represents a group of units; extract specific pieces of information from tables and lists.

databases

A database is an organised way of storing a volume of information so that it can be sorted quickly and systematically according to the details required. A telephone directory is a database. It stores information under alphabetical surnames. The information listed includes initials, possible business names, address and telephone numbers of the lines in an area. However it can only be accessed when the surname is known. Knowing a telephone number will not enable an address or a name to be found, nor will a first-name. Libraries maintain a cross-referenced filing card index so that books can be identified by author, title, subject etc. A computer database will reorganise the 'filing cards' in any way requested. Information has to be entered only once instead of once on each type of card in the filing system. The computer will also search the cards for any information that is requested. Obviously information must be entered in a way that the computer program can 'understand', so each program has its own way of asking for data.

Young children will consider the computer package 'magic'. They will not be able to appreciate the complexity of the sorting process if they are not introduced to databases via a concrete piece of apparatus such as a filing card system.

The National Curriculum expects children at level 3 to be able to "enter and access information in a simple database (possibly but not necessarily on a computer). However, young children should be creating and interpreting databases not linked to a computer before that level so that they begin to comprehend the processes and the questioning involved. Children will not be assessed as to whether they can "interrogate data on a computer database" until Level 4.

chart showing potential mathematics assessment by section

	water	soils, rocks and minerals	plants and animals	people and their communities	energy	climate	buildings, industrialisation and waste
number	4 6		1 3	2		2 3	2 3 4
algebra							2 4
space and shape	5	2 4		5	1		1 2 3 4 5 6
handling data	2 4 5 6	3	2 4 5 7	2 3 4 5	1 2 3 4	3 5	2 3 5 6 7
probability	2 4			4		2	
area	2						
capacity	1 3 6						
length	2 4 5		5 7	2 4 6	1 4		1 7
money	4			6	1 4		3
time	5		2		1 2 3		3
temperature						1	7
volume			4 6				
weight			6				